NOT A MARKETING TEXTBOOK

Praise for *Not A Marketing Textbook*

"Christina's extensive experience with start-ups and working with brands has enabled her to coach with a mind of an army general and execute with the skill of a sniper.

This book shows the importance of studying the target audience's persona to elicit the connection between marketing and human desires. It reduces so much guesswork for marketers trying to get the exact messaging to the marketplace.

This book provides vital consideration points for business owners to establish clear marketing key performance indicators. She has taught many what to do for marketing and how to execute marketing strategies better than many others.

Are you struggling to make marketing sense of your business or overwhelmed by the various marketing courses available out there? This book offers a roadmap and treasures of wisdom from Christina gained by practical experiences and case studies."

Andrew Chow, CSP
Chief Learning Officer, AP Academy Pte Ltd

"Veteran marketer Christina Lim's book, *Not A Marketing Textbook,* is a refreshing down-to-earth approach to demystifying marketing, and to providing practical and actionable building blocks for any business. Whether a start-up trying to create and define a new brand and territory; or an existing company looking to embark on a new direction and bring new products or services to market, the book is packed with practical ways to: position and define the brand correctly; make sure the idea is scalable; understand the customer and the competition; what to avoid; and last but not least, ensure the right team is onboarded. The stories and examples are relatable and inspiring to newbie or veteran alike, with many clever examples that prove you don't always need a massive budget to succeed."

Linda Locke
Author, CEO & Creative Director, Godmother Pte Ltd

"It takes a certain type of experienced expert that has the ability to translate complex principles into practical, easy-to-understand and just-in-time tasks in a way that does not dumb things down so much it becomes ineffective. Christina has done this for start-up founders in the critical area of marketing—an activity that cannot be ignored. This book is easy-to-read with relatable stories, structured in a way that helps one understand what's important to focus on depending on the start-up's current growth stage. Follow the advice, and you will find yourself laying the necessary marketing foundation your start-up will need to ensure sustainable growth and success. Well done, Christina!"

Dr Robyn E Wilson
Leadership & Strategy Expert, Mentor,
CEO of Praxis Management Consulting Pte Ltd

"Many start-ups fail because they do not know how to convert their ideas into businesses, Christina truly understands the challenges of start-ups from the inside. She draws from years of hands-on experience as a successful marketing leader to deliver practical and easy to apply building blocks that help start-ups jump over the hoops of branding, launching and marketing their businesses. This book is a must read for not just start-ups but also any businesses looking to navigate complex marketing and brand concepts."

Shirley Wong
Managing Partner of TNF Ventures,
Entrepreneur In Residence with Singapore Management University Institute of Innovation & Entrepreneurship

"I first met Christina in 2011 when she was Director of marketing for NTUC FairPrice, Singapore's largest grocery retail chain. I invited Christina to speak with my sales, marketing and customer experience team about how she had grown the social media presence for FairPrice in the very early stages of social media marketing.

She enthralled my team with her sharing. Thus inspired, my marketing colleagues went on to experiment with their own unique and engaging ideas. We eventually grew our social media footprint to emerge as a case study often quoted by marketing and advertising trade media.

Christina has that effect on people. She's a practitioner, not a preacher. Yet, she makes time to share and inspire. This book is peppered with her personal anecdotes as a marketer as well as best practices picked up from others which would make for excellent tips for those leading start-ups as well as marketers in established companies keen to pick new ideas and approaches."

Vivek Kumar
Chairman, Asia-Pacific Advisory Board, Global CMO Council

NOT A MARKETING TEXTBOOK

Practical Building Blocks to Launch and Grow Your Business

CHRISTINA LIM

Candid Creation Publishing

Candid Creation Publishing books are available through most major bookstores in Singapore. For bulk order of our books at special quantity discounts, please email us at enquiry@candidcreation.com.

NOT A MARKETING TEXTBOOK
Practical Building Blocks to Launch and Grow Your Business

Author   : Christina Lim
Publisher   : Phoon Kok Hwa
Editor   : Patricia Ng
Cover design   : Ryanne Ng
Layout   : Eda Miskom
Published by   : Candid Creation Publishing LLP
                 167 Jalan Bukit Merah
                 #05-12 Connection One Tower 4
                 Singapore 150167
Website   : www.candidcreation.com
Facebook   : www.facebook.com/CandidCreationPublishing
Email   : enquiry@candidcreation.com
ISBN   : 978-981-17173-9-0

National Library Board, Singapore Cataloguing in Publication Data
Name(s): Lim, Christina, 1968-
Title: Not a marketing textbook : practical building blocks to launch and grow your business / Christina Lim.
Description: Singapore : Candid Creation Publishing, [2022] | Includes bibliography.
Identifier(s): ISBN 978-981-17173-9-0 (paperback)
Subject(s): LCSH: Marketing. | Marketing--Management.
Classification: DDC 658.8--dc23

Dedicated to my beloved mother,
who taught me the virtue of grit,
and my dear daughter, Abigail,
who I hope will have the guts to pursue her dreams

CONTENTS

FOREWORD

WITNESS OF A BEAUTIFUL METAMORPHOSIS

I first met Christina at her office in 2009, when she led marketing at NTUC FairPrice, a heritage grocery retail brand in Singapore. Back then, my creative agency was appointed to develop their rebranding campaign.

Christina left a strong impression on me, and it was not only because of her distinctive facial features that makes one wonder if she was of Eurasian or Chinese descent. I was pleasantly surprised when she started interpreting creative ideas with a strong command of Mandarin. In that first meeting, I was impressed at how she had carried herself through the presentation with aplomb and intelligence, in the presence of senior stakeholders.

Our path would cross again when I was appointed onto the board of directors at NTUC FairPrice a few years later. There was always a presence about her, being highly articulate and professional at board conferences, she handled questions with great finesse.

Once, I was invited to sit in on a brainstorming session led by Christina, which involved dozens of people from different departments to develop brand names for a retail banner. Most of the participants had little or no experience with branding, but she was able to prepare them well in advance with information which helped to set the context for the discussion.

I did not expect the session to be any different from other workshops but I was once again amazed at her ability to manage the conversations across such a diverse group. Many workshop facilitators have the tendency to be biased as they attempt to guide the discussion; but Christina was different.

She had devised an approach that empowered everyone to speak up and skilfully drew potential ideas. She was quick at spotting potential sparks and guided the participants to build on them. It takes someone with a sharp mind to process ideas and connect the dots well.

I could see that she was respected by her colleagues and well-loved by her team; everyone had good things to say about her.

We had the opportunity to get to know each other more during a work trip in Taipei in 2016, during which she sought my advice as she was presented with an opportunity to join an advertising agency as a company leader. We talked about how the ad industry was in need of seismic change, and she was drawn by the challenge to inject new perspectives. At first, I thought it could be a backward move for her career to return to the creative industry after many years at a client organisation. I was also sad that we would inevitably lose a valuable talent and someone I really enjoyed working with.

Years ago, I left my job as executive creative director at BBDO, to build my own company which eventually got acquired by the WPP group. It took courage to venture out of the comfort zone into the unknown—I did not know if I was going to succeed. Christina was at that stage of her career where she was up for new challenges. To her, this was a potential transformation gig. And she went for it.

However, she was quick to assess the situation and decided it was not what she had signed up for. I was thrilled to know that she made a quick transition to join a new economy scale-up, honestbee, which was then growing their teams rapidly across multiple markets in Asia. She had always been drawn to the start-up sector and joining honestbee was her chance to gain a valuable insider view of new economy at work.

Undoubtedly, she adapted well to the dynamic environment, led young teams, and had to deal with a lot of ambiguity, typical of most start-ups. And yet, she was able to inject her brand of grace and apply her rich experience from the past.

From her writing, I could see that her time at honestbee, before the company spiralled into decline, was a season of exponential growth for her. She navigated the episode with a lot of tenacity and grit, and regardless of situations, she always manages to learn and grow from them.

That's what I really like about her.

The next time we had the chance to work together was in early 2020, where she was already a start-up advisor and CMO-In-Residence with Singapore Management University Institute of Innovation and Entrepreneurship (SMU IIE). We were in the same advisory board meetings for the 10th Lee Kuan Yew Global Business Plan Competition which attracted over 850 entries from start-ups, from 650 universities, across 60 countries.

This time, she was the seasoned and steady hand that guided the SMU IIE team in branding, marketing, as well as experience design for this international event. She is daring with her thoughts and highly agile in adapting the campaign around the challenges posed by the pandemic.

After reading her manuscript for this book, I was amazed at how she had been quietly amassing all this knowledge and wisdom over the years. Her experience and revelations are so inspiring that I ended up reading them twice.

In all my years in the creative industry and now serving on boards of big corporations, I have encountered many marketing leaders, talent like her who have an all-round hands-on experience in start-ups, large corporates, and the creative industry is a rare breed. What's more remarkable is how she has also excelled in academia.

Many marketing leaders have corporate experience but not agency experience, others have both agency and corporate experience but have not learnt to survive in a start-up environment. More often than not, many are airy and lack substance.

There is too much hogwash and too many fluffy theories on marketing in the world which confuse rather than help. Platforms, business environments, and market conditions will change, so right-sizing your strategy is at the core of making things work. Christina was spot on in her observations on the challenges faced by businesses when it comes to branding, marketing, and growing. She has demonstrated that she knows how to work the key nodes to help business ride changes.

The way a book is written can tell you a lot about its author.

In this book, you can tell that Christina genuinely wants to help people, not to show off. It was written with passion as she selflessly shares her experience and real battle stories. I am familiar with and was close to some of the cases shared.

This book is, like her, unconventional, pragmatic, and very inspiring. It is easy to read and it takes someone who truly understands the subjects to cut through all the jargon and distil complexities.

I believe that every book will find its own readers, and those who want to do well will be drawn to this book. While some companies may not be ready for her expertise, they may find this book a mind opener.

This book will speak to you and make you reflect. It can set you on the right track for your brand and business to grow.

Publishing this book is just one milestone in a promising journey that Christina has ahead of her. I have great faith that she is poised to impact many businesses in many markets.

Lim Sau Hoong
Acclaimed Creative Director and Advisor,
Board Director to listed companies

PREFACE

Which comes first—the chicken or the egg?

The reckoning of this popular existential question for my life happened in the most unexpected manner.

It wasn't when my parents discovered that I had won my first drawing contest at the age of eight, nor when I started beating my cohort in mathematics problem sums. The fateful event occurred at the end of my three-year university business administration degree education, in a humid afternoon on campus.

I was dragged into a packed lecture theatre tucked away at the corner of the school of accountancy, en route to catching a bus out of campus.

A team from the advertising agency network Ogilvy and Mather (O&M) was giving a talk titled "We Sell Or Else".

The agency had to answer a brief from their Air Canada client to sell the airline's routes to the travel agents in Singapore. This was back in the 1980s. There was no internet to buy tickets online, and people had to go down to the travel agency to book tours and flights. Back then, the in-flight experience left much to be desired. In-flight entertainment was limited, and most flights, until the mid-1990s, had smoking and non-smoking sections contained in the same space. It was, therefore, possible to be seated in the non-smoking section of the airplane, hiding under the blanket and choking from the smoke that travelled from the smoking section just one row behind.

Safety was a big concern. In fact, 1985 remained one of the deadliest years in aviation history as there were multiple air crashes. As such, Air Canada probably had to establish itself as a safe and reliable airline; they needed the travel agencies to sell their flights and be included in tour itineraries. The advertising agency's role was to get the message across effectively, and make an impression!

Fig. P.1: Handle with Care.

O&M designed a box to carry a tray of real eggs, with a label on the box that read "Handle with Care" (Fig. P.1). They deployed special dispatchers to personally deliver the eggs to all the key travel agents in the country. "Handle with Care" not only addressed the safety aspect, it also suggested thoughtful and attentive in-flight service.

The campaign certainly made an impression. I decided, there and then, that that was what I wanted to do for my career.

The answer to my career direction was the eggs!

I found out years later, from the creator of that campaign, that this became an apparent success with visible increase in flight bookings! It later went on to win some notable international creative awards.

Most see the visible parts of the advertising industry through the many great TV commercials, glitzy campaigns, catchy jingles, dressy ad executives, and flamboyant creative people. Like most outsiders, I was drawn to the glamorous aspects of the creative industry. Somehow, I managed to beat a panel of candidates in a group interview to win one of the two seats, to be an account executive at the award-winning boutique agency called Spencer & Friends.

No one saw the parts where we slogged away at wee hours of the morning preparing for a new business pitch, nor the daunting hours at the photography studio waiting for the photographer to set lighting for the perfect shots.

Nevertheless, I had some of the best fun working in the creative industry. It was as depicted in the TV series *Mad Men*, where the ones with the big ideas called the shots, where an ad with big white space and one-word headlines won awards.

MAD MEN GLORY

Along the way, technology crept in, in the form of computers and desktop publishing. I soon found myself developing static websites and digital ad banners. Those who were embracing new modes of advertising were leading new conversations at the client's board room. In the mid-1990s, clients were relatively uninformed about the change and relied on the advertising agencies to show the way.

The reason I was leading my company's first website project was because I had put my hand up in answer to a client's request to build a static website which looked more like a digital brochure. We had neither the expertise nor the experience to do that; we were just a couple of gung-ho twenty-somethings seeking a challenge.

Soon, there were no longer just advertising agencies. Digital agencies were just starting to spring up, followed swiftly by the transformation in digital media placement, enabled by a myriad of dynamic digital ad serving platforms.

The era of "Mad Man" was quickly evolving into the era of the "Math Man". The increased focus on data threw questions on the efficacy of conventional advertising now that the digital media usage promised better accountability in terms of performance trackability.

However, branding was slowly shifting online and onto social media and it was around this time that I crossed over to an in-house function on the client's side. I was excited at the prospect of finally being where I could see where advertising was delivering real impact to the bottom line.

JARGON GALORE!

Like many of my cohorts, I was taught that the road maps to (marketing) wisdom are built on navigating theories, frameworks, and case studies, with textbooks written by gurus in the league of Philip Kotler. Those, however, pale in comparison to the onslaught of planning tools, matrices, and jargon when I joined the advertising industry.

The advertising industry has a plethora of planning frameworks, "disruptive" and "innovative" methodologies, philosophies and yes, acronyms (TABS, 5Ps, 6Ss, 4Ds, and so on). Once the fancy packaging is removed, one would find that they are basically iterations of the same set of basic strategic principles.

Almost every advertising agency network claims their frameworks promise a path to eureka moments.

I am, by no means, trivialising the importance of these frameworks and methodologies. They are useful and can help organise our thoughts and ideas, and the senior management loves them on the merit that they provide some order and structure. However, they can also be confusing, rather than helpful, to the untrained eye.

Let's take branding as an example. Trying to explain brand vision, brand purpose, brand mission, brand belief, brand proposition, and brand positioning can be a real feat even for experienced marketers.

A CASE FOR SIMPLICITY

As I progressed with my career, conversations on marketing became more centred around driving desired business growth. That meant juggling multiple balls beyond marketing campaigns: growing leads, product efficacy, operation, service experience, etc.

In many of my mentoring conversations with the early-stage start-ups whose founders are not trained in marketing or branding, it helps to simplify marketing concepts, ditch the jargon, peel back the layers of packaging ,and focus on what matters. The typical marketing problems are mostly about getting noticed, getting trials, closing the deals, attracting repeat sales, retaining customers, growing revenue, and so on.

It is said that the principles of marketing are common sense, but getting the craft right takes training. Business builders, growth leaders, and start-up founders have other things to focus on such as winning the competition, stretching resources, managing business processes, developing products, etc.

There has to be a simpler way.

What if I could show, not just tell, the useful fundamentals towards building go-to-market strategy? Stories, analogies, and visuals are great ways to do so, and I will be sharing some. Some of the company names mentioned in the case studies have been anonymised to focus on learning principles instead of the status of these businesses.

I have penned this book as an extension of a recurring Ready-for-Market masterclass which I developed and conducted for start-up incubators and early-stage start-up founders. In fact, my original intent was to write a book that could be read in a series of 60 minutes, the working name for it being "60-minute Conversations".

This book is part experience-sharing and part thought-starter. Instead of being a textbook, it is intended as a conduit of mentoring conversations with me, covering more than just marketing, but without the paddings of complicated marketing concepts and jargon. Even though the book would take longer than 60 minutes to chow through, it is designed to be an easy read.

Let's un-textbook, shall we?

INTRODUCTION

In the summer of 2014, I had my first encounter with the start-up community that fuelled me with new inspiration for my career and ignited new fire in my belly.

I attended a three-day immersive online retail summit with representatives from the Asian regions which included, among others, Thailand, Indonesia, Vietnam, and Hong Kong.

Back then, I was leading branding and marketing for a home-grown grocery retailer from Singapore, NTUC FairPrice. As an established leading grocer, it had multiple retail formats under its wing, including an online store. The summit was a great opportunity to exchange ideas with players who were knee-deep in the e-commerce space and I was eager to learn how we might embark on the emerging online retail journey.

It was refreshing to meet the founders who were mostly in their twenties and thirties, casually clad in their start-up branded T-shirts, jeans, and sneakers, all with special sparkles in their eyes.

My admiration for these people rose when I learnt that many lacked the luxury of resources in big marketing organisations and had to bootstrap their operations at the early stage of their business, working with limited capital and resources.

One Vietnamese online book retailer founder shared that he started his business because Amazon was not available in his country; he had his bedroom piled with books and had to pack them for fulfilment right on his bed. Another founder of an online grocery start-up in Indonesia had to personally handle his first few deliveries on his motorbike because he could not afford to hire delivery riders.

I was drawn to their passion and the energy they put into their ideas and visions. Their mindset and resoluteness were a stark contrast to my colleagues in a large retail chain struggling to make e-commerce work despite having better resources.

For the years that followed, I continued to keep a keen interest in that community, like a child on the outside of a toy store, always looking in.

Four years later, I had the opportunity to join a Business Transformation and Innovation Program organised by the IMD Business School ,where part of the programme included a study trip to Bangalore, otherwise known as the Silicon Valley of India and a hotbed of Indian start-ups.

During the trip, we met with a number of start-up founders to learn about their innovation journeys. The visits opened my eyes to space outside the box of the corporate cocoons we had grown too familiar with.

The start-up world is a fascinating space because they create the future, new economies, and new industries. It is the hotbed that births new ideas, new business models and innovations that solve real-life problems. I once delivered a career talk in school for students interested about the start-up world. When the students were asked about their curiosity about start-ups, they unanimously cited the desire to change the world for the better.

QUICK STEPS TO ADRENALIN

In 2018, when I was approached to join a three-year-old scale-up, honestbee, I jumped right into it. After all, it was my opportunity to experience start-up in a front row seat! In retrospect, I wanted a slice of a business that was changing the world with the gig economy.

At that time, it had rapidly expanded into eight markets with multiple business verticals. The company had begun recruiting experienced specialists to inject much needed structures to improve efficiency and depth of knowledge. I was privileged to have within my cohort, highly experienced veterans who were the best of their craft in retail business, user experience, product technology, customer service, and data science.

Even though honestbee was growing in size, it was still running at the cadence of early-stage start-ups. It did a lot of right things to make things happen and had launched new services, it was also spending exceedingly to acquire new customers.

Like many early-stage start-ups, they had to grapple with multiple issues in order to succeed. Not only did they need to roll up their sleeves to make things happen, they had to make their business last. They had to progress beyond their many minimum viable products and skateboard initiatives, and also build the right foundations to keep their business financially sustainable while it scaled and expanded rapidly.

Start-up mentors and investors listed the top drivers behind start-ups succeeding in commercialising and these include the following:

- Ability to attract the right investors and raise funds;
- Ability to build a scalable business model;
- Availability of a sizeable addressable market (globally or regionally);
- Having a solution to solve a big problem;
- Ability to build a formidable and complementary team;
- Resourcefulness and resolve to execute their business ideas;
- Engine to sustain traction for growth; and
- Swift product roll-outs ahead of competition.

For a period of two years after I left honestbee, I served as a mentor and CMO-in-residence (CMO is Chief Marketing Officer, by the way) with the Singapore Management University Institute of Innovation and Entrepreneurship (SMU IIE), where I engaged and mentored many early-stage start-ups under its incubation programme, through scheduled consultations, masterclasses, and hackathons.

A diverse spectrum of subjects was covered beyond marketing as many start-ups I spoke with needed help to define their business fundamentals and sharpen their business models. In reality, most business go through the following, different stages (Fig. I.1):

1. Ideation;
2. Development of MVP and Prototyping;
3. Launch;
4. Acquisition of Customers; and
5. Growth,

and the needs at each stage vary.

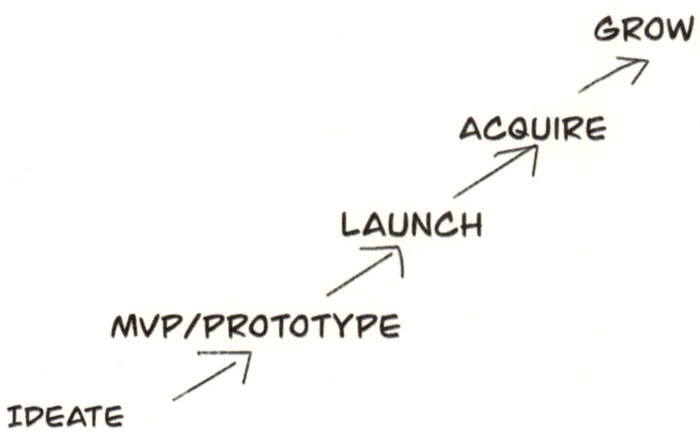

Fig. I.1: Stages of a start-up business.

Working with the start-ups kept me grounded and on my toes. It was, nonetheless, invigorating; everything from its people, their passion towards solving real-world problems, and their cadence to make things happen. I continue to discover new respect for these brave souls who dare challenge the unknown and chase their dreams.

I count it a privilege for me to live vicariously through the experiences of the founders whom I mentor and the companies I advised. Most importantly, playing as an accomplice in creating a new and better world.

This is the new creative industry!

BUILDING BLOCKS TO GET STARTED

Whether you are at the stage of product development, pre-revenue, ready to launch, or have already commercialised and are now working towards growth, your needs at each stage vary.

Whatever your needs are, I will be providing you with thought-starters and basic building blocks to help guide your thinking towards creating and refining your go-to-market strategy.

This book will provide you with some foundational components to start you on your journey to build your vision of a new and better world.

Chapter 1 contains some useful tips on how to build compelling pitches for your business, whether it's with potential investors, strategic partners, or potential employees. Chapters 2 and 3 touch on branding matters, with examples and simple guides on how to create your own brand stories.

Chapter 4 highlights the importance of doing adequate study of your potential customer segments and suggests different approaches to triangulate your customer study.

In Chapters 5, 6, and 7, you will get more illustrative perspectives on building your funnel strategy and your engine for continuous growth. For the marketing folks looking to recalibrate their strategies, read this as easy refreshers and learn to cut to the chase and make things happen.

In Chapter 8, I share some valuable lessons on developing and marketing budgets, as well as how I had managed to optimise marketing investments with revenue targets in sight.

Chapter 9 shows what to measure and report on your marketing ROI (return on investment), while Chapter 10 delivers simple frameworks to build your marketing capabilities—when to hire and when to train.

The chapters are organised sequentially to help build the right foundations. While it is possible to read these at one go, I would recommend that you pace it out.

In order to get the most benefit out of this book, take time to reflect and participate in the Classrooms and Checklists segments at the end of each chapter. Thereafter, you may return and zoom in on specific chapters for more in-depth study.

CHAPTER 1

TALK ABOUT YOUR BUSINESS

"Tell me about yourself."

This is probably one of the most commonly asked questions at job interviews. And typically, people go straight into talking about what they do and have done.

Likewise, "Tell me about your business" is one of the most commonly asked questions when start-ups pitch for funding. Whenever I asked the same to open my 60-minute mentoring sessions with start-up founders, most of them spend half that time explaining what they do. In the multiple pitches I sat in with angel investors and admission pitches for start-up incubators, many early-stage start-ups fumbled to find the right narratives on their business ideas and struggled to finish their pitches within the stipulated 4–10 minutes allowed.

Why is this the case?

Understandably, most founders have invested a lot of effort to develop their venture from initial inspirations, designing product offerings and business models. As such, many dwelled excessively on the operational details of their businesses and the product features.

Product ideas and service ideas
are not business ideas
unless you can identify customers
who will pay for this.

Until you can demonstrate there is potential for economic value exchange for your product idea or service idea, it is just an idea.

Your mobile app does not
constitute a business idea;
it can be a business enabler or
a channel for your operation.

Quest is a start-up that runs a marketplace matching errand runners with people seeking help for their errands. The service seekers and service providers are called "citizens" and "heroes", respectively. They centred their business idea pitch around an app that would cost a hefty investment to build.

However, it was more important for them to deliver a solid business case and demonstrate steady traction for their pilots. Their business can work by enabling the errand matching using mobile web or even Telegram at the start. This should be where they devote their investments. Their good business traction would put them in a much better position to convince investors to fund the building of the app.

A great vision is not a business idea.

A number of start-ups have mentioned that they aspire to "build ecosystems", some wanted to "create cult-like brands", and others promised to deliver generic promises of "better quality of life". Whatever their destinations, they all need to start with tangible offerings that people are willing to pay for.

VALUE PROPOSITION MATTERS FOR YOUR CUSTOMERS

Winning the mind and heart of your potential customers demands that you successfully convey how your business adds value to their lives.

> Your value proposition answers the question:
> "What's in it for me?";
> it states your role in the life of your
> customers, how you solve real-life problems.

There are many products out there that do not solve real problems. Social media is inundated with videos of life hacks and solutions, some of them are simply brilliant, some funny, and others are just weird.

Khaby Lame, a Senegalese-born TikToker and Instagram influencer from Italy, became a social media sensation in 2021 when he started creating a series of TikTok videos in which he silently mocks overly complicated and somewhat stupid life hack videos, from taping fork so it can be used to drink soup, to a gadget for holding down the rest the pizza while one peels off a piece for consumption. In his video, Lame responded to these life hacks and gadgets with a wordless shrug and often while looking exasperated.

Granted, some of these original "life hacks" were just created for entertainment purposes, but Lame's reaction videos show how often we can make life more difficult or complicated than it is necessary. For many of these gadgets, the inventions were often redundant.

While Lame's TikTok videos might have brought us some light moments and chuckles, ironically, they reminded me of quite a number of pitches which failed to convince me on their reasons for being. A common trait among these are inventions or solutions with no real apparent needs, nor does it solve any problem.

CB Insights, a market intelligence platform, did over 100 post-mortems on failed start-ups to address the burning question of "Why do start-ups fail?" They have discovered that as much as 42% of start-ups failed due to "lack of product market fit or no market needs". The top reason why start-ups failed to take off has to do with insufficient validation done on business ideas resulting in poor market adoption and fit.

Quite a lot of my mentoring conversations with start-ups may start from the need to fix their acquisition and launch ideas, we eventually circled back towards value propositions.

Without clarity of the intended addressable market segments and their needs, it would be challenging to construct their sales pitch or start to engage their target segment. Most early-stage startup founders believe that they have great products that people want. However, that's not always the case.

There are also other start-ups who are driven by ideas or the excitement towards a new technology.

Telling people that you have a great product doesn't make them want it.

This applies to any business, not just start-ups.

We were taught, in school, the importance of unique selling points or unique selling proposition (USP) to show how a product or service is different from the competition, with the obsession about "unique" features and attributes, believing that it would convince customers to convert. In reality, even if you have an awesome product with all the great bells and whistles, if it doesn't help customers or if it's unable to explain its value clearly, people won't buy it.

Most of the start-ups that struggled with pitching for funding lack a clear value proposition, as such have the tendency to fumble. A strong value proposition needs to come before you talk about unique selling points. At its website, *Strategyzer* has a useful framework for developing value proposition: it aligns what the business offers to the customer's needs. The value proposition canvas is presented as one of the key components to business model design and it advocates the need to understand customers' needs (Fig. 1.1).

As a consumer, I am unwilling to fork out money to buy any product and service if it's not relevant and meaningful for me.

Fig. 1.1: Align business offerings with customer's needs.

Let's look at an example.

While a lot of people might be in need of styling advice, hiring a personal stylist is not an obvious action. The service of a personal stylist is deemed to be the privilege of the affluent, celebrities, and for special occasions. And these are conventionally high touch services and are not usually affordable.

Inspired by her own needs, Alyssa created a social styling platform, GS, that serves as a marketplace for C2C (consumer-to-consumer) personal styling services, and it runs on a mobile app. GS tapped into influencers and the social community. Customers needing styling advice are able to access and be matched to a crew of professional stylists located from around the world.

Alyssa wanted to serve the "everyday girls", not just the affluent group. She wanted to democratise personal styling and make it more affordable, which is possible since it's done online with her app-based styling platform.

This is how Alyssa could adopt the value proposition canvas to sharpen the design of her offerings and create a strong proposition that appeals to her target segment. Doing this well requires an intimate understanding of the market you are serving and showing empathy towards your potential customers. To do this properly, Alyssa would have to do her homework and speak with potential customers.

According to the value proposition canvas, the customer "jobs" could be functional, emotional, or social. Hence, the jobs for the "everyday girls" could be:

- Functional: I need to dress for the occasion.
- Emotional: I want to be confident.
- Social: I want to look smart and sharp among my peers.

Customer "pains" refer to any undesired costs or situations, negative emotions, or unwanted risks encountered in achieving the customer jobs. For example:

- I have nothing to wear.
- I have outdated items in my wardrobe.
- I have no time to shop.
- I have no idea how to put together a look for an occasion or to project a great impression.

The customer's desired gains are essentially the "ambitions that people have that would ultimately make them happy". For example;

- Getting a curated look and fashion advice for the occasions they are dressing up for.
- Getting validation from their peers—the same reason why girls like to bring a friend along for their shopping trips.

The value proposition canvas would force Alyssa to dive deep into what is truly meaningful and valuable for the customer. She would probably discover that the "everyday girls" want more than just styling; they also need help to build, curate, and upcycle wardrobes. By understanding the profile of her potential customers in terms of their pains and needs, she would land herself on a bigger addressable market which now includes people who might not be just looking for styling. There is a greater opportunity in her business towards solving the wardrobe problem, not just styling, even though styling could be a key differentiator. She needs a sound business model to make sure the services take off, potentially supported by a repertoire of partners, beyond fashion brands and stylists.

GS's offering to address the customer pains and gains can include the following:

- Access to a panel of fashion styling expertise from around the world;
- Marketplace for curated merchandise;
- Wardrobe curation service;
- Styling tips on fashion;
- Reference to curated looks from global retail partners.

This example shows that by thinking through the value proposition, not only could you sharpen your proposition for your potential customers, you are able to gain better clarity on developing your pool of potential partners and business collaborators.

A big red flag is when a solution is looking for a problem that does not exist.

Conventionally, the best solutions are the ones which are inspired by addressing actual gaps in the market. There should ideally be latent demands for products or services to close these need gaps.

Dragons' Den is a BBC show that gives budding entrepreneurs three minutes to pitch their business ideas to five multimillionaires who are willing to invest their own cash, time, and expertise to kickstart a business. In one episode, two hopeful entrepreneurs pitched their "poo-product" called Wype, an innovative serum that turns normal dry toilet paper into eco-friendly wet wipes.

According to the scientist-turned-founders, the product was "specially formulated with 99% natural ingredients" and when sprayed onto regular toilet tissue, it would instantly turn it into an efficient "100% biodegradable" and genuinely flushable toilet wipe. The two were on the mission to refine toilet time.

When asked about the difference between Wype and other competitors with similar claims of turning tissue papers into wet wipes, they defended their product by saying that their bottles were made of aluminium instead of the plastic, thereby making them "more premium". They also felt that they had an eco-friendly angle that others did not leverage on.

Was there a valid value proposition with Wype?

When 90% of the population in the UK didn't consider this a problem, there was no real customer pain.

Toilet papers work just fine and besides, there are other alternatives that do a better job to cleaning the bottoms, such as water, or even the more expensive Japanese branded Toto toilet system that comes with water spray and air-drying function.

Wype will not eliminate the use of toilet paper so it doesn't make it any eco-friendlier. In addition, an assumed premium in the form of an aluminium bottle delivers no real value add and is not meaningful. In fact, a lot of brands blindly pursue and promote unique selling points that are not relevant.

One member of the panel summed up a glaring problem: "To raise awareness for a problem that maybe 90% of the population (in the UK) didn't realise existed, and to change consumer buying habits is going to take millions of dollars in marketing spend."

The creator of Wype obviously needed to reframe the problem and proposition and first get better insights on what the consumers really think and expect.

Shirley Wong, the Entrepreneur-in-Residence with the SMU IIE, shared her experience on her years of reviewing pitches from many early-stage start-ups:

"Starting with a solution first can sometimes feel like fitting a square peg into a hole.

"There are solutions that are not made to solve the market problem. I've seen this before and can't pinpoint one instance where there has been a positive outcome.

"These teams are so obsessed with creating novel technology that they deprioritise validating market needs. Although given enough time and options, there will invariably be instances where solutions can find problems to solve, it is far less likely than a problem being met head on by a solution, since the solution was developed to solve that exact problem!"

"Sustainability" has been a popular angle on which start-ups build their business ideas, nothing wrong with that. I have personally mentored a few and I would always advise the importance of staying connected to customer needs and to make sure that their products really work. Without which, your "sustainability" agenda might only serve as a differentiator and help create appeal, but would not constitute a main reason to buy.

Customers want the product to solve their problems, whether it's moisturising their skin or cleaning the floor, and they want your solution to be simple to understand and easy to use. Consideration on whether it is produced with eco-friendly ingredients or ethical methods, comes thereafter.

Protenga is a biotechnology start-up big on the food sustainability agenda. I had the opportunity to work with its founder and CEO Leo Wein to refine his pitch for funding. Essentially, Protenga leverages insect technology to help farmers and food companies produce better and more natural food in more sustainable ways; these companies are able to reduce waste of their biomass by turning them into sustainable protein. And because the Protenga systems are modular, its technology can be deployed in a decentralised and cost-efficient manner.

Protenga can squarely build their brand story on the sustainability agenda because there is a real need for sustainable food production;

THE MORAL OF GREAT BRIEFS

In talking about any idea, it pays to be concise. If you need many words to describe something, chances are, you are still trying to make sense of it. In the world of attention deficiency, being able to articulate and get to your point fast, means you have better chances of getting your audience interested in what you have to offer.

One of my earlier trainings while I was in the advertising industry was writing creative briefs for developing advertising that sells.

As an account handler, we had to interpret and distil client's requirements, often convoluted and unstructured, into one-page creative briefs. These would guide the concept development of the required marketing communications.

Birthing the "single-minded message" proved to be one of the most tedious feats a junior advertising person had to undertake.

Think about it, if you have only a split second to arrest the attention of someone on the street who is in a hurry, you really need a message to stand out and make them stop in their tracks. The single-minded message in the one-page creative brief sums up the most important thing you can say.

One of the ad agencies I worked for mandated that this field should not contain more than 14 words. This process made one think long and hard about what really matters. You would think it's easy to come up with a maximum of 14 words. Not so.

The 14-word message needed to ignite and inspire the creative team to birth great ideas. If it's not good enough, one would expect the brief to be thrown out of the creative department.

In another instance, my client at Citibank in charge of Car Loans planned to send a group of partner car agents for an incentive trip to Hawaii, in appreciation for helping to achieve record sales for Citibank's car loan.

The client's brief to us was indeed "brief" and functional. We were given an itinerary of the proposed trip and the task to make the recipients excited.

I thought that would be a breeze—who wouldn't be excited to be invited for a free trip to Hawaii?

A literal 14-word single-minded message could read: "Citibank invites you to join us for an incentive trip to Hawaii!"—that's 12 words.

But it wasn't good enough. The clients were two rather flamboyant gentlemen and were expecting more than just a beautifully designed invitation card. The invitation had to be an extension of their personalities and it needed to make an impression.

After hours of word grinding, I mustered all that I had and came up with: "Aloha, it's how we say thank you!".

I also remarked in the brief that the client did not want to see any invitation card design. Needless to say, the creative team lapped up the opportunity to do anything unconventional.

At the end of the day, each of the invited sales agents received a big box with a label which read "Gentlemen, lift your skirts!"

In the box was a handwoven blue-grass skirt, in the dark Citibank blue, with a printed wrapper featuring a fictional story of how an ancient Hawaiian King Wamehameha celebrated his battle victory with a game of stick and coconut which evolved to be the modern-day golf, dressed in the ceremonial grass skirt. In the same way, Citibank was inviting them to re-enact the victory dance at Hawaii in an incentive trip with games of golf in its itinerary.

Two months later, the client sent us a group picture of the delegates at the golf course, all wearing the blue grass skirts.

That piece of work went on to win an award at the prestigious New York Festival award show, in the later part of that year.

Here's one more reference. Once we were asked to create a campaign for a media owner to convey the effectiveness of their out-of-home media network.

We were provided with statistics on the media network's high viewership. Of course, success of an outdoor campaign depended on more than just the media network, content played a critical role too. As such, we had to design a campaign that not only conveyed the benefit, but also captured the attention of pedestrians.

Writing an ad featuring only numbers can be boring. The single-minded message was simply written with just one word.

This was another award-winning campaign which featured a forensic evidence bag containing bloody eyeballs. Its headline read "EVIDENCE!" while its supporting body copy detailed the viewership in terms of eyeballs garnered.

One-page brief and 14-word single-minded message writing provided one of the best trainings during my ad agency days. It is beyond wordsmithing, doing it right requires focus, clarity of thought, and sharpness in communications. It takes discipline and focus.

CLASSROOM

ACING THE PITCH

Doing a pitch well involves more than just the content you deliver. Here is a simple guide for you to build your elevator pitch.

1. Think about your audience.
   - What do they hope to gain from your pitch?
   - What are the potential reservations and preconceptions you are about to propose?
   - What do you want them to take away?

Potential investors and partners want to be convinced that you have a sound business model. As such, you would want to tick these boxes:

- ❑ What are the problems your business helps to solve?
- ❑ Where are your addressable markets? Are they sizeable?
- ❑ How does your product or service work?
- ❑ Do you have interesting technologies and customer experience that will make your business a game-changer and hard to copy?
- ❑ How would your business make money?
- ❑ Why should they part with their money for a stake in your business?

Then, write out your answers to these questions.

2. List the potential reasons they would say "no" to you and take every "no" as an opportunity to improve your pitch.

3. How are you differentiated from other start-ups?
    Investors may sometimes listen to multiple ideas from the same category with solutions addressing the same problems you have identified. You need to show how you are serving the same customer segment better. Are your products more effective? Is it easier to use?

4. Condense
    - By now, you would have lots of relevant content to work with but you need to fit it into a few minutes allocated for you.
    - Apply the discipline to distil what you want to say—try condensing what you want to convey in a paragraph into two to three sentences.

5. Construct
    - Organise your talking point into a logical flow like how you would tell a story, within the time limit, of course.
    - Script your pitch before you construct your PowerPoint slides. The slides should work for your pitch, not the other way round.

CHAPTER 2

BRAND MATTERS

When I was asked by a client from China to explain the value of branding, I referred to a chapter in the famous book *Art of War* by Sun Tzu, an ancient military strategist. The chapter talks about Shape (形) and Situation (势), the two basic factors that determine the outcome of a war.

Shape refers to the tangible factors that are objective, stable, and easy to see such as the actual military strength, its external manifestations of the weaponry, and preparation for war.

Situation refers to the more subjective, changeable, and contingent factors, such as war strategy, deployment of the troops, the courage and morale which can affect the potential of the troop.

While it is logical to deduce that the size of the troops determines the victory or defeat of a war, there are many battles in history in which a small troop won the game. This is where Situation had come into play.

A good military strategist considers multiple factors such as location, climate, environment, diplomatic relations, resources, timing, etc., in order to devise winning battle strategies that best optimise the Shape of the troop.

Another illustration of Shape and Situation at work was found in the classic novel *Romance of the Three Kingdoms*.

It was a famous story of how Zhuge Liang, a military strategist during the ancient Chinese three-kingdom era (AD 208–209), who fooled his opponent by playing to the Shape and Situation principle. Zhuge Liang received a military order to secure 100,000 arrows within three days so they could be used against the strong Wei Army—a seemingly impossible feat.

Back then, the two opposing forces were separated by a river near the Red Cliff, a strategic battleground. Zhuge Liang asked for more than a dozen straw boats to be prepared, each mounted with dozens of straw men clad in military uniforms. He then waited till the third day when there was thick fog on the surface of the river, before advancing towards the enemy. He figured that Cao Cao, the general of the opposing Wei Army, was afraid of fraud and so would not venture to investigate, but instead would choose to shoot their arrows into the mist of the river. He was right (Fig. 2.1).

Fig. 2.1: Zhuge Liang's plot to get a new supply of arrows.

Zhuge Liang created the illusion of an invading force, without deploying any troops but fooled the Wei Army into supplying the arrows he needed. In this episode, Zhuge Liang played brilliantly by leveraging his understanding of his competition, the conditions on the battlefield to create information and psychological mind games to gain the upper hand.

The Shape in this episode were a dozen grass boats with straw men. The Situation he had successfully created was an advancing army.

The Shape and Situation analogy is my regular go-to story to explain what branding is and the importance of it.

BRANDING RIGHT TO COMPETE

Likewise, when branding is done right, it can deliver a similar impact. Smart branding is what empowers a new market entrant to be favourably placed to win the battle against the stronger incumbents. It is all the more important for start-ups entering the play.

I observed that the bulk of the most commonly asked questions during mentoring are related to packaging themselves right to go to market. Branding plays a critical role for B2C (business-to-customer) brands, as they need to compete in sometimes saturated market segments. Right-placed branding would set you in the right posture against your competition and enhance your appeal towards your target customers.

An interesting book on branding is *Eating the Big Fish* by Adam Morgan. This book zooms in on challenger brands who are neither the leader nor incumbent in their category. Despite the humble states of their Shapes, they have business ambitions bigger than their conventional resources. They are prepared to do something bold against their giant incumbents, breaking existing conventions or codes in the category, in order to stand out. These brands created Situations to break out.

In the book *Beloved Brands*, author Graham Robertson talked about branding as a competitive strategy and how it potentially evolves across different stages of its market entry, stages of growth, types of consumers, and competitive environments.

> A brand gives meaning and value to what you are selling and good branding gives you the upper edge.

Getting this right would help you develop your brand story and narratives, so as to captivate the attention of potential investors, partners, employees, and customers. In the chapters that follow, we will look at just how to do that.

BRANDING CAN INCREASE PERCEIVED VALUE

When luxury fashion house Balenciaga featured Arena—its extra-large shopper tote—in its 2017 runway, many took a double take at its close resemblance to the iconic Ikea blue shopping bag. Apparently, the bag designer Demna Gvasalia was indeed inspired by the famous blue bags' longevity and functionality.

Of course, the Balenciaga version of the giant shopper tote is made of blue wrinkled, glazed leather and carries a gold-stamped logo as well as a price tag over $2,000, compared to its humbler version from Ikea.

This was not the first time that Balenciaga had pushed out bag designs that look like expensive copies of cheap carriers. Their earlier creations included the Blanket Square handbags that resemble Indian *kambal* bags and the Bazar Shopper Tote which take inspiration from cheap market bags. Yet they were somehow able to command super premium price tags. The gap between the designer bag and the commoners' favourites—though they might be made out of better-quality materials—lies in varying perceived brand values.

The market bag, Indian *kambal* bag, and Ikea blue bag are functional reusable carriers, while Balenciaga's giant bags are luxury fashion accessories. Needless to say, they appeal to different groups of people.

> Brand strategy provides direction for the company to position itself, define its competitive set, and potential tracks for innovation and product road maps.

VALUABLE BRANDS

The brand I had worked on was ranked among the top as "most valuable brand".

What does that mean?

According to Forbes, the formula for tabulating the value of the brand takes into consideration the revenue of the business as well as earnings before interest and taxes (EBIT), averaged over three years. It also takes into consideration the impact the brand plays in each of their industries.

Another brand value measurement I had looked at was the brand equity metric by AC Nielsen, which compares how a brand fares against its competition within the same category. There are four factors that contribute to the score for brand equity:

- Would your customer travel further to find you?
- Would they pay more for your product, especially if there are other me-toos?
- Would they buy your product and services again? (Efficacy of product, experience, friction, customer service, ease, and accessibility)

- Would they recommend you? (Experience and efficacy, customer service)

> Brand value affects what makes one
> choose your brand instead of others.

The benefits of branding investments may not be immediately tangible as it affects different aspects of the business such as sales, customer loyalty, and advocacy.

There are many more methodologies out there to rank, categorise, and score brands and getting branding right does have an impact on the earning potential of a business.

When most start-ups launch their offerings, the immediate priority may be to define an addressable market, get market validations, and secure funding, instead of branding.

Nonetheless, branding right will help you to command pricing, build appeal for your product and services, and eventually acquire customer following.

BRAND AS A PERSON

So, what is a brand?

"If your brand was a person, how would you describe this person?" This is a common question posted by brand consultancy companies to understand how consumers perceive a brand. Respondents would be asked to provide a more vivid description of this brand person—its age, gender, potential occupation, personality, and values.

When I first joined a retailer years ago, we had just completed a brand audit where respondents were asked to describe our brand and our competitors' brand as brand persons. Our brand was being seen as a businessman dressed in suits and who drove a BMW. Our main competitor, on the other hand, was seen as a friendly middle-aged uncle with whom one could sit down and have a chat over coffee at the heartland coffee shop.

For a brand who had always prided itself as a homegrown brand that cares for the people, we were not perceived to be approachable and even somewhat disconnected from those we wanted to serve. The competition appeared to be doing a much better job in being relatable.

Hence, if a brand is a person, it would have multiple dimensions to its being and it can leave an impression to those it meets. If you want to be remembered favourably, it is important to learn how to construct your brand person.

THE WHO OF YOUR BUSINESS

We are not referring to celebrity or brand mascot, although if there was to be one eventually, it should align with its desired image. Sometimes the "mascot" is in the person of the founder, like Steve Jobs for Apple and Elon Musk for Tesla.

> The brand person is how you want your
> brand to relate to others.

I have worked with young companies and start-ups who are steadily growing and want to start developing their brand narratives and guidelines. Many found themselves stuck in the confusing maze of brand terminologies—brand vision, brand mission, brand belief, brand purpose, brand values, core values, brand persona, brand Ideas, and so on. If it's of any consolation, experienced marketers struggled with these too.

Most people are able to describe the tangible attributes and experience of the products and services that they consumed. The concept of a brand, however, may come across as abstract. When asked to describe a brand, most will lean on visible brand attributes such as its logo, name, packaging, and signature colours.

Personifying a brand means to construct the perceptual concept of how your brand would look, talk, and act, just like a person.

Take IBM and Apple as examples. You would probably see the IBM-Brand-Person as more of a corporate person while the Apple-Brand-Person as one who is more creative.

Sometimes we hear a name and immediately conjure a mental image of what this person might look like and that image is often shaped by things we have read or past experiences.

The concept of mental imagery was first consistently used in the discipline of empirical psychology. It plays a crucial role not just in perception, but also in memory, emotions, language, desires, and action-execution.

Let's dive into the various dimensions of a brand person.

What would your brand person think?
What would your brand person's beliefs be?
What are your brand person's aspirations?

At the age of 15, Greta Thunberg protested outside the Swedish parliament to pressure the government to meet carbon emissions targets. Her actions started a global movement where more than 20,000 students—from the UK to Japan—joined her to protest the global failure to arrest climate change. A year later, she sailed across the Atlantic to attend a United Nations climate conference in New York and delivered her famous speech:

"You all come to us young people for hope. How dare you? You have stolen my dreams and my childhood with your empty words."

Her speech won support from climate activists, scientists, and public figures, and inspired the world, and she went on to receive a Nobel Peace Prize nomination.

This climate campaigner's belief is that her generation and the ones that follow do not deserve a sick planet. Her personal mission is to drive real action for climate change. With this belief and mission, she envisions a future for the world where we have a healthy planet, and where everyone plays their parts in keeping it that way.

Likewise, when you start to think about your brand as a person, navigating the mission, vision narratives will become easier. Beliefs and vision could inspire actions, and in the business context, the offerings and experience you deliver, the partners you collaborate with, the people whom you hire, etc.

And you would want these to support and align with your goals. This deals with the soul of the brand—the one that people connect with.

CAN OTHERS TELL YOUR BRAND APART FROM THE CROWD?

The world has no shortage of character impersonators, some for fraud and others for entertainment purposes.

I once had to be dressed up for a company costume party. I went for the complete deal—black latex full bodysuit with high heeled boots, a whip, and cat mask that severely restricted my range of vision. My boss, who sat next to me, was supposed to be a rock singer. He asked if I could see my food as he couldn't through his long wig.

I couldn't, but I had to stay in character.

All the discomfort became worthwhile when a young daughter of a fellow colleague asked me, "Are you Catwoman? I saw you in the Batman movie!"

I was no Catwoman, nor was I an agile fighter; but I dressed the part.

Likewise, do you (your brand) look like the rest of your competitors, like one of many masked men in the movie, *V for Vendetta*?

When I consult for companies on their branding, I would place their brand assets in the company of all their competitors, so as to assess if they stand out from the pack or blend into the sea of sameness.

There exist some category branding norms. For example, the dominant use of red among insurance players, green and blue for healthcare companies, popular use of dots and circuit nodes as graphics for technology companies, etc.

A brand's "look" goes beyond the logo design. It affects all relevant touchpoints consumers have with your brand. This can include packaging, uniforms, the store front, the design of your social media platform and website, etc.

Now think about your brand person (Fig. 2.2):

- How would this person act and talk?
- How would your brand person relate to your customer and community?
- Would your consumer want to be seen with your brand person?

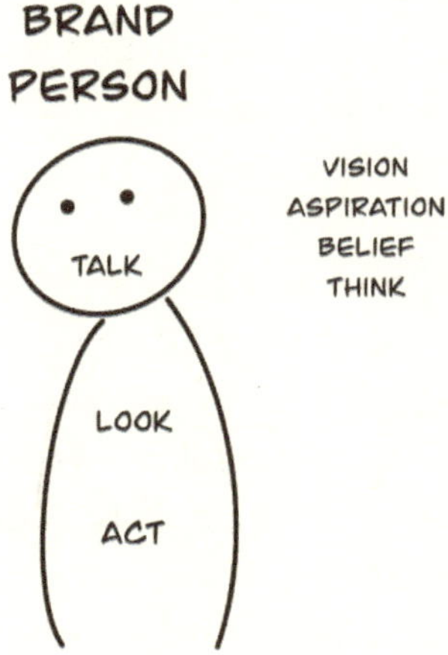

Fig. 2.2: The Person of the Brand.

It is logical to deduce that if you are serving affluent customers, you would probably want to dress your brand to look "premium".

Many would agree that Rowan Atkinson's portrayal of Mr Bean was a class act, even though he had had other memorable characters in the Blackadder series. The non-speaking character of Mr Bean by Atkinson came out of his interest in physical comedy, where he portrayed someone who is clumsy and naïve of the world around them and capable of causing disaster.

Hence, it would take more than dressing up to impersonate Mr Bean because he is characterised more by his demeanour, gestures, and behaviour.

Likewise, how your brand behaves has to do with how you (the brand) talk and how others experience you. Your customers and prospects would have many touchpoints with your business. Will they find you consistent and raise their comfort level over time, or will they find you schizophrenic?

Guidelines on brand identity, communication, and user experience design are some of the hygiene practices among more established brands. They guide brands on how they should act, talk, and look.

Branding is fun. When done right, it would help your brand differentiate in your category and enhance your appeal. It all starts by constructing your brand persona.

LESSONS FROM THE BEST

When we look at the world's top 10 most recognisable brands— Apple, Google, Amazon, Microsoft, Coca-Cola, Samsung, McDonald's, Toyota, Disney, and Mercedes Benz—we can always attach a meaning or image whenever any of these names are mentioned.

For Apple, its products—iPhones and iPads, to Apple Watches and iPods—are owned all over the planet. Its brand logo of a bitten apple has evolved from the original colours of a rainbow to the current monochrome black; that helped to establish Apple's reputation for minimalism. The most notable part of the Apple brand would have to be its iconic leader, Steve Jobs.

For Amazon, its logo is the word "Amazon" with an arrow going from the first "a" to the "z"—conveying that the company sells everything from A to Z. This is a perfect reflection of the brand's value proposition.

Google's name is ingrained in the minds of anyone who has ever used its search engine. The current logo is the word "Google" colourised in blue, red, yellow, and green. According to Google's design blog, the "e" at the end of the logo is at an angle to suggest that the company will always be a bit unconventional. I love the "Google Doodles", which are customised throughout the year. It calls out days of significance, as well as to commemorates the achievements of people on their birthday.

For McDonald's, the golden arches have been its icon and have not changed for over 50 years. One associates the brand with happy meals and happy times with the family.

For Disney, it is recognised largely due to the popularity of its movies, theme parks, as well as its characters like Mickey Mouse, Cinderella, and Tarzan. It is now a major film-maker and one of the largest media companies in the world.

WHAT'S IN A NAME?

Name is a big part of a brand and it will conjure up images and associations, something of what the company promises to deliver. The Singapore grocery retailer I worked for is called "FairPrice". It instantly clearly conveys the promise to deliver good value and affordability, and it aligns with its social mission to "moderate the cost of living".

The right name can make your brand memorable, help people understand your intent, and even create positive vibes towards you.

I wasn't born as Christina. My given name in Chinese originally means "precious red stone" in the Chinese Hokkien dialect. My grandfather named all his granddaughters "precious"—my sister is "precious diamond" and my younger cousin is just simply "precious treasure".

I used to think these names were tacky and old-fashioned, but these names carried the hopes and best wishes upon the christened. My grandfather, even though he was a little bit patriarchal in his thinking, considered all his granddaughters as precious and worthy to be cherished.

I later added Christina to my name in high school as it was easier to remember. And it was trendy then to have a Christian name, even though I wasn't one back then.

On a lighter note, my aunt in Malaysia had ten sons and a daughter. All of her boys have "Kim" as a middle name, which means golden, akin to prosperity. So, their names go like this: Kim Seng, Kim Leng, Kim Meng, and so on. And when it came time to name her youngest and eleventh son, she ran out of ideas for names and my cousin was eventually called "Kim Eleven". It's funny but true, and I could understand her predicament. In fact, there were many Chinese families in older China, especially those from rural villages and unlearned, who would name their children by numbers.

In the movie *Dances with Wolves*, Union army Lieutenant John Dunbar, who fought in the Tennessee civil war, was sent to the distant outpost at Fort Sedgwick. He decided to stay and restore the fort as it was deserted and in disrepair. During his time there, Dunbar encountered a wolf with two white feet and attempted to tame it. He named it "Two Socks".

He would later befriend a Sioux man, a native American tribesman. When the Sioux observed Dunbar and Two Socks chasing each other, they give him the name "Dances with Wolves".

The movie fascinated me beyond being a thoughtful and expansive story flanked by breathtaking scenery of the Wild West. I was intrigued by the names of the characters: Kicking Bird (Sioux man), Wind in His Hair (Sioux warrior), Ten Bears (village chief), Stands with a Fist (white woman), etc. There was a story behind each name which sparks your imagination. For example, Stands with a Fist could probably point you to someone who is defiant or tenacious.

Some names are predictable in their category.

The few robotics companies which I mentored carried names that end with "–botics". While the name may suggest which category it is in, how each brand differentiates from the rest, however, is not apparent.

Let's take a leaf from the superheroes naming convention. Most heroes get their names from their appearances, for example, Superman, Batman, Wonder Woman, Catwoman; or their superpowers, such as Spiderman, Flash, or Mystique. Now, imagine if Thor is not called "Thor" but John; would he be believable as the powerful god of Asgard?

Some names are cute and others invoke curiosities.

I think it would be nice to be able to tell an interesting story about your name, even to stand out from the competition.

Take Apple for example. It's an unlikely name for a tech company but I immediately like it. It is uncomplicated, approachable, and it certainly stands out from the rest of its more serious competition.

NAMES THAT FIT THE HAND LIKE A GLOVE

I came across many interesting names among start-ups. Some provide clues on the nature of their business, what they do, and the benefits they deliver. Some are just pure abstract. Here are a handful of examples of hardworking names:

Rushowls

They are a dynamic bus-pooling company offering timely and affordable shuttle rides. Its name sounds like "rush hours" which suggests it serves the needs of commuters during the rush hour madness.

Beauty Undercover

They collect customers reviews as well as provide independent reviews on beauty and hair salons in Singapore. "Undercover" suggests mystery shopping which provides unbiased reviews on the salons' performances and service quality; that association evokes trust. Even though their review methodologies are somewhat different from mystery shopping.

KpopKart

This was a start-up by a group of K-pop enthusiasts who created an online commerce platform. KpopKart enables K-pop lovers to market and sell custom-made K-pop merchandise. The name immediately draws the eyeballs of K-pop lovers.

Crunch Cutlery

This start-up creates edible cutleries packed with flaxseeds, chia seeds, and whole wheat, promising a boost of nutrition.

Have you ever thought of how Google and Facebook got their name? Facebook was literally created as a campus networking platform. It's literally a "book" of the faces you might see around campus.

Google started off as a search engine named BackRub because their search engine searched through backlinks. The founders figured that BackRub wouldn't work as a technology company name and further changed it to Googolplex. Googolplex actually refers to 10 to the power of 10. Eventually, the founder decided on the shorter form in "Googol". A misspelling incident in trying to search for a potential domain name had it typed as Google and that was it. Not only was the name unique and memorable, it carries with it an interesting story. It is also important that the platform technology and experience work, otherwise Google could potentially have a negative connotation.

Landing a good name for your business, innovation, and products, sets you in the right direction to stand out, get noticed, and be appealing. This is especially true for start-ups operating in uncharted space.

HOW TO CREATE A NAME

Over the past 20 years, I have led multiple naming exercises, for product names and retail banners. Here is a simple approach for brainstorming and developing a brand name.

The exercise would usually start with a half-day workshop. You would want to involve some key stakeholders as well as participants who fit the profile of the potential target segments.

There are three easy steps.

Step 1: Rev Up
- Align all participants with a simplified overview of the product and value proposition, keeping it brief and succinct.
- Start mental warm-ups by getting participants to think of multiple groups of words associated with the defined proposition.

  For example, let's assume the proposition reads "healthy dessert for summer". Invite the participants to generate different groups of words associated with "summer" and "dessert" respectively. These word groups could be in categories like colours, words, objects, feelings, animals, plants, numbers, and even shapes. You may create as many groups as you want.
- Organise each group of words on multiple flip charts or clusters of post-it pads.

Step 2: Randomise
A few years ago, I had the opportunity to visit the David Bowie exhibition held in Tokyo. Bowie was, no doubt, one of the most impactful music artists in the 1970s and 1980s. In a documentary clip made in 1997,

he shared about a sentence randomiser app which he had designed to write lyrics for his 1995 album *Outside*.

He called it the Verbasizer.

With the program, he would take a sentence and divide it up between columns. Sometimes it would be three to five sentences, and other times more. He would randomise and mix the words from different columns, from different rows of sentences, and he would end up with "a real kaleidoscope of meanings and topics and nouns and verbs all sort of slamming into each other."

He explained that, for example, he might pick up something like "The top kills himself" and he could build a story from there. He might interpret "top" as the boss, and suddenly he might have a picture of a boss in his 30s, throwing himself out of the window in the Great Depression. That could spark him into building on that story and eventually writing a song around it.

Our Randomise phase builds on a similar methodology to what David Bowie did with Verbasizer. Likewise, we can start mixing words from different word groups that were generated in the Rev Up phase. For example, mixing one word from the colour group and another from the shape group. We might end up with new combinations, such as "orange circle" or "pink bubbles".

Remember how you are asked to create names on Facebook by combining, for example, the colour of your shirt and the last thing you ate? So, I might come up with "black noodles" or "blue apple".

As this progresses, new ideas can be birthed from those. You may also consider merging the words to form new ones, for example, evolving "Blue Apple" into "Blupple"'. Be open-minded and have fun.

Step 3: Reality Check and Refine

Once divergent ideas are generated, they need to be converged, sorted, and reviewed for a shortlist. The shortlists can be put through some filters where we consider:

- **Relevance:** What are the norms in the business, community culture, and social taboos in your market? Are there essential values that you can hinge on? Are they against potential cultural and social taboos? For example, black and 13 may be considered ominous.
- **Reference:** What are some predictable terminology and language of the trade? How are the competition and other players in the same category named? Which of the shortlists could be adopted, avoided, or ditched?
- **Resonance:** Could these appeal to your target segments? Check for negative reactions, understand why people hate it, and find ways to address them. Also, test the potential names with key stakeholders to identify any affinity or negative emotions.

By now, you would have landed on some finalists

- **Review:** Do they stand out? Are they memorable? Are you able to build interesting brand stories around them? Can they be trademarked? Are there URLs with similar names in the markets and countries you intend to operate in?

    Continue to refine and scrub your options. This is where you can start to involve designers to help you visualise and build a mood board around the names to show how the potential brand names could morph into logos or even inspire packaging ideas.

Naming work involves both science and art. It is a very necessary step to get right, in order to be ready for market.

CHAPTER 3

TELL YOUR (BRAND) STORY

We all learn through stories, analogies, parables, and fables. Stories help to provide contexts where the storyteller and his audience can connect. Good stories convey more than facts, they make ideas and experiences familiar, which engage their listeners, build trust and rapport. Stories can trigger our imaginations, inspire us to discover, reflect, and be creative.

American photographer Brandon Stanton started a movement for personal storytelling when he launched his photoblog titled *Humans of New York* (*HONY*) in 2010. The original *HONY* featured street portraits and interviews collected on the streets of New York City, which eventually developed a large following through social media. He subsequently added to *HONY* portraits and interviews collected in nearly 20 different countries. Thereafter, every major to minor group of people jumped onto the "Humans of …" bandwagon, and emergence of "Humans of …" for many other cities followed suit.

Stanton's original intent was to focus on the storytelling and his portraits captured intimate stories of strength, addiction, redemption, regret, and love.

There is something about personal stories dotted with vulnerable subjects with imperfect lives that deliver credibility and authenticity. His storytelling activates the emotional appeal and connects the subjects with their audience.

A good brand story helps others connect
with your brand.

Brand stories can be harvested from a sea of perspectives, personal experiences, and ideas. My conversations with start-up founders and business leaders have enabled me to uncover hidden gems on the stories behind their innovations and why they have set up their business.

A well-crafted story doesn't need too many words and it can contribute to a compelling pitch.

THE BODY SHOP STORY

When I first discovered The Body Shop, I was drawn to its green-painted wooden facade and its honest, down-to-earth packaging. I was a big fan of their body butter and body scrub.

When I later read about the belief of Dame Anita Roddick, the founder of The Body Shop, I truly became a fan of the brand. The Body Shop was one of the pioneers in prohibiting its products to be tested on animals and they promised that their ingredients are ethically sourced and naturally-based. They even published this promise on their website to further demonstrate their commitment.

Roddick believed that business could be a force for good— The Body Shop had promoted fair trade with developing countries very early on. As the default ambassador of the brand, Roddick was an activist in campaigning for environmental and social issues.

A story like that helps a brand like The Body Shop stand out from the rest of the pack. It conveys moral values that coincide with the consumers' and the current trends.

Brand storytelling is not just for big brands.

Use brand storytelling to humanise your brand so that it's easier for people to align themselves with it.

There are different ways to tell a brand story and, contrary to perception, they do not have to be tear-jerking in order to win hearts and connect emotionally. However, they should not be too detached from your business.

One of the commonly asked questions I have encountered has to do with how to tell a brand story for technical products or B2B (business-to-business) services.

Let's look at some examples from companies I have mentored.

For a logistics company that provides delivery and fulfilment services for fresh produce farmers, they can celebrate the farmers' hard work in bringing forth the beautiful produce of the land. They can show empathy by identifying with the farmers on their challenges to run their business and present the company as enablers.

Similar approaches work for other e-commerce logistics companies who want to serve the last mile fulfilment needs of small-scale e-commerce sellers, by simplifying shipping.

For SaaS (software as a service) companies, building brand stories on the success of its customers have always worked.

For a company who produces and sells special craft beers, it can humanise the brand by sharing stories of how the brewing art originated, or the human story of those involved in the brewing process. The background context can add to the premium of the brand.

For a company that adopts intensive R&D (research and development) processes and technology to produce sustainable cleaning products, they can appeal to the corporates and consumers' rising concerns on sustainability by highlighting how easy it is for them to play a role.

For a company that detects subtle movements in facial features in real time, using machine learning and artificial intelligence, appealing to decision makers in governmental sectors would need a different take. Playing the emotive card would not work. Instead, it could focus on fuelling a vision for efficient immigration operations or investigation accuracy of law enforcement bodies, etc.

The key to finding good brand stories is to look for the sweet spot where the brand values overlap with the customers (Fig. 3.1).

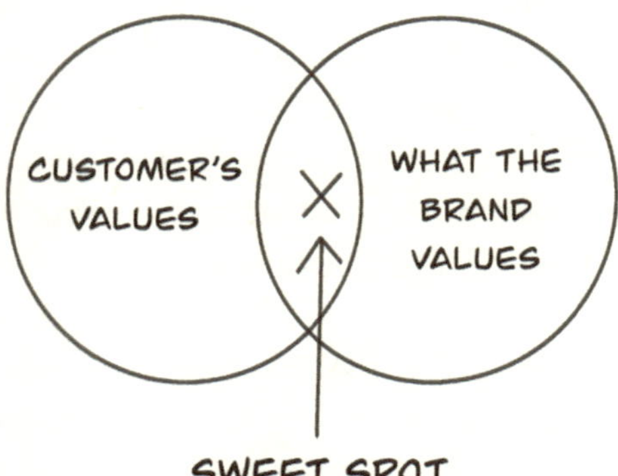

Fig. 3.1: The sweet spot for good brand stories.

Success of the customers is a highly probable route for storytelling. You can humanise your brand by telling stories of the people in your world, such as your business partners, your employees, etc.

These stories can be told using different mediums such as blogs and videos, you can share them on your LinkedIn profile page and your website, you may also embed them in the communications to your potential leads. These are great for uniting and building believers among your internal stakeholders.

You might ask: Isn't this also content marketing? Yes, it is. Brand storytelling is part of content marketing. Content marketing is simply the marketing tactics where you use content to sell, engage customers, and tell brand stories.

CASE STUDY: TELLING STORIES OF BRAND HEROES

When most people think of branding, they immediately expect some kinds of key visuals and emotive TV commercials. However, consumers can be sceptical about what brand says about who they are. They would rather believe what others, including strangers, say about the brand.

In 2015, Singapore celebrated its 50th birthday under the banner "SG50". This was a momentous event for Singaporeans to reflect on how far they have come together as a nation and people. Many brands rallied behind the national milestone to join the bandwagon of their respective nostalgia trips down memory lane.

NTUC Fairprice is a home-grown brand that most Singaporeans grew up with. It has stayed true to its social mission to moderate the cost of living and has been integral to the nation's growth through the years. As the leader of its branding efforts, instead of talking about its contribution, we decided to break the mould by adopting a different approach—we chose to celebrate unsung heroes.

The branding initiative was named "For the Heroes in Our Lives" and we invited Singaporeans to share stories of the unsung heroes in their lives. This was a branding campaign that was not brand-centred, but community-centred.

We first created a platform that rallied people from all walks of life to join the celebration. In doing so, we projected our values by inviting the nation to celebrate unsung heroes in their lives.

The movement was led by a series of four films featuring:

- Muthu Kumarasamy, a passionate union leader who devoted his life to improving the lives of the union members who are public daily-rated workers, an often neglected and marginalised group of the society;
- Kit Chan, a Singaporean singer and actress who had made a mark in Asia, and the original singer of one of the country's favourite national songs, "Home";
- Yip Pin Xiu, Singapore's gold medallist for swimming in multiple paralympic games and regional para games; and
- Zulkifli Baharudin, a reputable business leader and local humanitarian leading Mercy Relief in Singapore.

We invited each subject to talk about the unsung heroes of their lives. For Muthu Kumarasamy, it was his elder sister who took care of him as a mother would; for Kit Chan, it was her primary school teacher, Ms Kang, who shaped the way she sees the world; Yip Pin Xiu paid tribute to her mother for being the constant pillar of support in her journey; and Zulkifli Baharudin was inspired by his religious leader in his humility and generosity.

In addition, we also told stories of people in the world of NTUC Fairprice, featuring real stories of employees. We used their stories as mirrors to reflect the values that the brand embraces.

The difference between a good and a bad brand lies in whether it can win hearts and minds. While it helps to have a budget for your communications campaigns, share of spend doesn't always equate to the share of mind and share of heart.

Brand should look at achieving the **share of mind** from its audience by cultivating longer time spent with the brand, and **share of heart** by creating deeper emotional connection and engaging.

I hope this case study inspires you to find an interesting angle to tell your own brand stories, whether it's to the media, your investor, business partners, customers, or potential employees (Fig. 3.2).

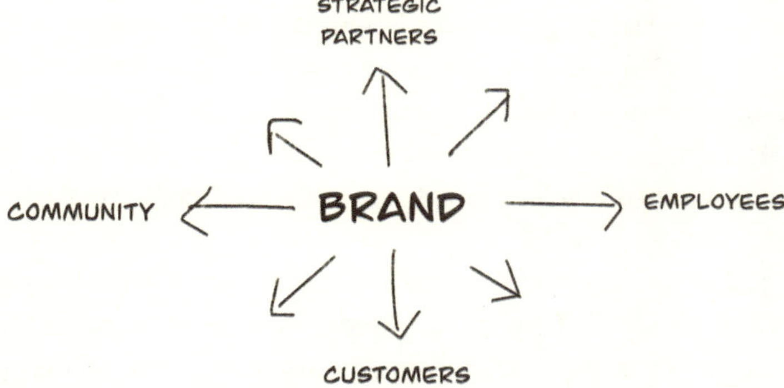

Fig. 3.2: Different angles to tell your brand story.

DEVELOPING BRAND NARRATIVES

Brand narratives are the building blocks for your brand stories.

The first steps to developing brand narratives involve interviewing the company's executive leadership teams, which could also include board members and advisors. The intent is to gather and align perspectives on:

- Where the company or brand is currently; and
- Their respective aspirations for the future of the company or brand.

I once worked with a health entrepreneur, Julina Halim, who is a trained nutritionist, wellness coach, as well as experienced Pilates and tango instructor. She speaks in conferences on health and wellness subjects; she has also made multiple television and radio appearances in Asia where she has given advice on wellness.

Julina was planning to launch her own brand of wellness therapy for women's health and recovery programmes for people with movement impairment. She needed clear narratives for her own personal brand.

I got her to pen discovery notes on the "why" and her thoughts about what she is doing. Her discovery notes totalled over 10 pages, in which she talked about her personal passion for dancing and how her revelation on dance inspired her to develop her own signature therapy for Parkinson Disease recovery, using tango moves. She also advocates that women's independence start with strong bodies.

Julina had multiple sources of inspiration for her therapies which serve varied groups of people—the movement impaired, women after birth, mature women, etc. Her story points were found in her personal experiences or events that shape her beliefs and personal values, and how she was inspired to create therapies.

Julina finally landed with R.E.A.L. as her key brand narratives. She advocates that "wellness is about making R.E.A.L. choices in everyday lives to be at our A game" and she invites all to "Get R.E.A.L. with Julina".

R.E.A.L. in her brand narratives refer to Rest, Eat, Act, and Live, in which she is perfectly placed to lead. These narratives work as her brand manifesto.

Let's consider another example.

Gabrielle was planning for her own wedding, but being a complete newbie to the world of cosmetics, facials, and spas, scouting around for the right service providers turned out to be rather frustrating. She went through some hoops and loops to accomplish her goals after encountering horrifying ordeals, bad service experiences, and crook practices.

Her journey inspired her to create a review platform to share the outcome of research on these service providers, as well as invite people to provide honest reviews of the beauty salons they have frequented. Gabrielle wanted to help others like her who are struggling to find the right help to transform themselves beauty-wise but who are potentially vulnerable at the hands of dishonest merchants.

On her website, she shared a heartfelt and personal story of how she founded her business, her beliefs, struggles, and challenges, that could resonate with the people she hopes to serve through the review platform. Her story carried three key attributes that makes it engaging:

- **Make it personal and authentic**

  She shared her own encounters, the good, bad, and ugly aspects of her struggles and challenges;

- **Make it relatable and believable**

  She provided context of her problems similar to what her target audience would have experienced.

- **Make it meaningful**

  She drew the associations between her solution and her belief of enabling every girl to transform.

HOW TO DEVELOP YOUR BRAND STORY

Brand consultancy firms might conduct workshops to collate and align such inputs using a combination of fancy tools and methodologies to help them decipher and uncover insights for potential brand narratives.

In the absence of a brand consultant, there are some basic steps to guide you towards finding gems to develop your own narratives.

Part One: Mass Mining

I run similar drills with start-up founders using a pared-down version of the brand discovery process. The respondents are asked to contribute their thoughts with guiding questions such as the following:

- What triggered you to start your business, or to innovate?
- What are the problems you intend to solve?
- What are your aspirations for yourself and for your business? (This is where you start looking into the future.)
- What are your personal beliefs associated with your business?

In the event where I am not able to facilitate group explorations, I would encourage them to write their own discovery notes. Similar to how fishing boats pull a fishing net through the water behind one or more boats, we focus on capturing raw and spontaneous thoughts. And it's alright to have multiple iterations of the same thoughts in the same notes, which could be later curated and organised.

Part Two: Find the Hidden Gems

Once the thoughts and ideas are collected, the fun part of discovery begins. This is where you review your notes and start organising the thoughts. Here's how:

1   Sieve out duplicates and repetitions.

    The same ideas could be articulated in different ways. You are likely to find critical building blocks for your brand narratives among these.

2   Group similar thoughts into themes and blocks.

3   Look for story points that are personal, relatable, and meaningful.

4   Find a common thread to string different story points together.

Part Three: Craft Your Story

Once you have identified your story points, the fun part is where you start crafting your (brand) story.

Remember the 14-or-less example shared earlier? Your story should not read like a novel and it should be easy to understand. Modify the length to work with the mediums you are using.

Curate the angles and tonality and have versions for investors, your potential customers, or even your staff. It helps to share your draft with someone you trust to get feedback for refinements. You might want to engage a skilled writer to help finesse it.

In their feedback, ask:

- Is it easy to understand?
- Is it inspiring?
- Does it come across as authentic?

Here are some things to note when building your brand story:

- Be authentic.
- Make it relatable.
- Go beyond your attributes and benefits.

- Speak in your customers' language.
- Inspire and motivate.
- Show empathy.
- Try not to be too abstract.

Once done, you can feature your story on your website or even on product packaging. Sometimes, this could present interesting angles to build your PR (public relations) story.

CHAPTER 4

KNOW YOUR CUSTOMER SEGMENTS

Among the things early-stage start-ups must do in order to be successful with their go-to market, business ideas and market validation sit at the top of the list. Most start-up mentors and investors agree that many start-ups are not doing validation correctly and sufficiently.

WHY ASK THE CUSTOMER?

One of the most famous quotes on driving true innovation attributed to Henry Ford is this, "If I had asked people what they wanted, they would have said faster horses." (Fig 4.1)

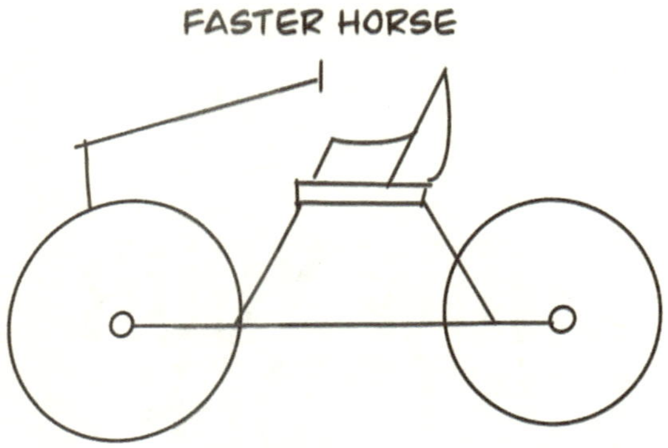

FASTER HORSE

Fig. 4.1: Ford's solution to faster horse.

This was used to support the notion that true innovation should be done without customer inputs. Steve Jobs had also been referenced as advocating that companies should not rely on market research.

Specifically, Jobs's quote reads, "Some people say give the customers what they want, but that's not my approach. Our job is to figure out what they're going to want before they do ... People don't know what they want until you show it to them. That's why I never rely on market research. Our task is to read things that are not yet on the page."

These were often misunderstood and misquoted as the rationale for innovators with solutions looking for problems.

While customers may not know they need an iPhone before it was created, they might have the needs that the iPhone can address. Hence, customers do know what they want, they just don't know how to articulate it. We do not know if Henry Ford asked the customers; but if he did, they would have told him they needed faster transportation, but would be unable to specify that they need a combustion engine.

As such, customers may not always be right on telling what they want in the actual features, but they can tell you what benefits they are looking for and how they want that to improve their lives.

Hence, the key to finding the answers is really in asking the right questions.

Here is a checklist of questions to assist you when you do your market validation:

- Is there a real problem or need that your product can solve?
  Often, start-ups are in a rush to start work on the idea without full appreciation of what the market really wants.

> "We often encounter start-ups that are so obsessed with their own ideas and technology that they struggle to find potential use cases for their products."
> — Start-up Mentor

- Are there visible demands for your solution?
  The Kickstarter crowdfunding platform is a great way to assess if your product can attract demands from your desired target segment, before more funds are poured into the venture. You might also uncover new segments that may be interested in your solution.

> "Hustle for pilots in the target segment. Make sure that you test the response with the right target segment"
> — Angel Investor

- What does your competitive landscape look like?
  Some start-ups do not scan the competitive landscape sufficiently. Beyond scanning the presence of other competitors who might be providing similar solutions, you should also

assess how the target segment is addressing their needs with substitute solutions.

Competitive landscapes may vary across different geographical regions and different target segments.

- Is there willingness to pay for your solution?
  Your intended price point would take into consideration the cost of development and cost to go to market. If the perceived value of your solution does not level with the price point, or if the product is not affordable, then you are not going to get any sales.

> "High level of interests in your product
> does not equate willingness to buy."
> — Angel Investor

- Is your business idea feasible to implement?
  There are uncontrollable factors in your value chain, such as reliable sources of raw materials, political risks, and regulatory compliance requirements, that can all hinder your plan to commercialise. It is not uncommon for businesses to bring untested solutions into the market; bigger companies are guilty of making that mistake too.

There are other methodologies that can help you add depth to the understanding of your potential target segments.

ASKING QUESTIONS BEYOND THE WHATS

Famous philosopher, Socrates, said: "True wisdom comes to each of us when we realise how little we understand about life, ourselves, and the world around us."

Throughout human history, we have always been fascinated with the world around us. We questioned the who, what, why, and how of life and business.

I am personally very curious about how people think and feel, and how these trigger what they say and do. Therefore, it is no surprise that my favourite subjects in school were consumer behaviour and psychology.

Over the years, I have participated in different ways of mining insights and accumulated valuable hands-on experience. There are many things we can measure if we think hard enough, and many ways to do so.

I invite you to think beyond the conventional quantitative and qualitative research methodologies that are taught in business schools. For start-ups that are bootstrapped to launch your business, investment in commissioning formal research can be hefty investments.

We cannot assume that Steve Jobs and his teams did not capture the needs of their potential customers. The fact is they are all users of the products they designed. They might not have engaged in market research as we know it.

In order to understand if you have got the right WHAT that people want to buy, we need to first understand the WHY behind their buying decisions.

In our earlier chapters, we touched on the importance of value proposition design, doing it right requires us to gather insights, not observations; it means going beyond the demographic and statistical references on market potential. You do need to embark on some primary studies.

HUMAN EMPATHY STUDY

With design thinking becoming more mainstream, many organisations are increasingly incorporating this technique of innovating into transformation journeys. It isn't dissimilar to how the creative industry generates ideas—just more scientific and methodical.

I love how it advocates starting with understanding latent needs, emotions, and feelings of its potential customers. The principle of design thinking aligns with how I was trained in direct marketing, where I had to dissect what people think at a granular level.

The design thinking discipline starts with uncovering inspirations, empathy study, followed by ideation and implementation. I had personally utilised this in the ideation of digital transformation projects.

In empathy mapping, we observe our subjects (such as our consumers) in their environment—what they feel, think, say, and do. We strive to understand what the consumers' pains and gains are in getting their jobs done. These jobs can be functional, emotional, or social.

Substantial amount of information can be gathered at this stage to shape your understanding of the users' needs, which are eventually used for your product and service design.

You probably have more than one group of would-be customers for your products. Simply, walk a mile in the shoes of your potential customer segments and you will discover that the needs and wants would vary for each of your defined groups.

USABILITY TEST

There were times where the product and design team can be too intimately involved in the process that they forgot to check what it's like to experience the product for the first time.

Likewise, services could be designed to address the organisation's operation constraints or processes, but they might not be aligned with how customers would use it. There might be different ways to use the service according to different people's preferences on lifestyles, good service, and product design to take into consideration.

At honestbee, their delivery and shopping apps were used to enable the delivery and shopper contractors in the field. The apps helped them in order management, job task management, and delivery management.

To make sure that they accurately captured the user requirements, the experience design team shadowed the shopper and delivery contractors in the field during their shifts. These direct interactions with the field workers helped them to acquire an accurate contextual understanding of the usage context. They could improve work flows and user experiences on the working apps with the insights gathered.

Likewise, for any consumer facing app or platform, we can adopt a usability test when we need to introduce features and experience. There is nothing like testing it with real people. Real consumers can be invited to try your prototype (app/web) products—give each of them specific tasks and invite them to think aloud as they experience the product, explain the rationale on their actions. In that way, you can capture in-the-moment considerations.

A lot of times, your customers may not understand what you have to offer until you show it to them, especially when it is something new or something they are not familiar with.

It is the same principle as when we sample food in the grocery stores or sniff the fragrance strips in the duty-free stores. Except that the prototypes used are samples before the product is actually manufactured, for piloting in smaller groups. The groups should ideally be representative of the potential target segments, so that learning can be derived from how they respond and interact with it.

While it is common to track typical web/app usage data such as the time spent per session and numbers of sessions per transaction, these data do not reveal the reasons for those usage behaviours. Uncovering the motivations (the WHY) behind those actions calls for direct interactions to mine in-the-moment and contextual insights.

These are not your conventional methodologies for customer study but I do find them really useful references for helping to triangulate the problem and needs of your target segment.

Let's look at an example.

Jane loves the vibrance of Asian tribal prints and thought it would be great to wear these. She decided to launch her own line of fitness outfits carrying these prints. She thought it would be good to start small and implement these prints onto the fitness apparel category.

She subsequently engaged printmakers in the tribal community to supply her with the print designs and also found a factory that agreed to produce samples for her apparels.

She planned to sell the line of fitness apparel through a website created just for her brand as well as at an e-commerce marketplace. As a millennial, that's how she shops for her clothes most of the time, online.

At this point, Jane has relied on her personal preference and experience to conceive her venture. She has ascertained how it can be designed and manufactured, the potential cost, and lead time of development.

However, in order to be ready for launch, she needed to do groundwork on the nature of demand and competition.

She immediately searched online for similar products on the online marketplaces and discovered that the sportswear category she had initially set her eyes on is highly saturated with many players, with rather diverse offerings. Some attires are sport-specific, others are specialised athletic performance wear that are often dominated by specialty brands.

Since she lacked the capability to design the sportswear for "performance", she decided to rely on her aesthetic prints as the main appeal for buying her tribal-print sports apparel.

In scoping out her potential addressable market, she found that there were limited statistics in her secondary research to help accurately size up the market potential. However, she might still be able to get some data points from insiders in the category such as the garment manufacturers and key retailers. She could also study keyword search trends on Google, on e-commerce sites, etc.

In reality, sportswear is evolving from exercise wear into leisure wear. The term "athleisure wear" has, in fact, been coined to refer to athletic apparel which people can wear in non-athletic settings. Thus, Jane needed to reframe her market boundary, with reference to the athleisure sector. This sector is fuelled by technological innovations in fabrics, the trend of sporty aesthetics, and the promise of enabling body beautiful movements.

> At this point, Jane has yet to uncover any insights on preferences of potential customer segments because she has yet to define her target segments!

She needed to define her target segments beyond just demographics, which she loosely defined as active women aged between 18 to 45 years old. She had a general idea of what her target segment would wear her apparel for, based on her own reference to people in her world.

Here's how she can adopt the human-centric studies shared above to help her hone her go to market products.

By defining a handful of potential target segments, she can start developing persona for each of the segments. For example:

- "Active Annie" who lives an active lifestyle, or 'Trendy Trisha" who is easy-going, sociable, and loves to include sport apparels into her OOTD (outfit-of-the-day), etc.
- For each of those, Jane can start to shape each persona by attaching demographic and psychographic profiles, to make these come alive.

Jane can start interviewing a handful of people who fit into her identified personas to understand their respective buying journey and experience.

- By diving deep into how they think, feel, act at different stages of the buying journey, the type of channel they get information from, and probing the reasons behind those responses, Jane would gain valuable insights on the more latent needs, struggles, and preferences.
- She can also test the appeal of the design, material quality, form factor, and even how much people will pay for her product. She can use these insights to help her find pivot and refine her go to market product.

Jane might also discover the not-so-obvious channels, such as fitness centres. There are multiple channels she can activate to get exposure for her brands and plan her future marketing programme to tap on potential sources of multipliers, such as fitness instructors who can promote her product.

The next thing for Jane to do is to produce a small batch of apparels to test the market. Until she proves that there are interests and visible demands for her apparels, she is unlikely to build a strong case as validation to convince investors to fund her.

Therefore, she should focus on identifying target segments that deliver quick wins and on which she can build her beachhead market. She should also think about how she can activate this segment to spread news about her products

Christina Teo—Chief Builder at she1K, the world's first C-suite executive angel syndicate—has seen her fair share of pitches from early-stage start-ups. She shared that: "Many start-ups are unable to demonstrate decent market validation for their business ideas, nor show real evidence of a sizeable addressable market. Many did not make the effort to engage in real customer conversations or even get their beta products tested with the right target segment. They fail before they have the chance to actualise their product."

CLASSROOM

CUSTOMER JOURNEY MAPPING

Building customer journey maps for different industries and categories can help you to gain a better understanding of unmet needs and underserved gaps. This methodology involves one-to-one conversations with people at different stages of the customer journey.

There are many tutorials for this to be done professionally and here's a simple way to start building your own customer journey map

First, lay out the stages of your customer journey: Trigger, Research, Purchase, and Post Purchase (see Fig. 4.2).

Then deep dive into the each of the stages to flesh out the customer's goals/jobs:

- what they think;
- what they feel (the highs and the lows);
- what they do;
- what their pain points are.

You can use this excellent framework for more comprehensive questioning for a defined target segment. Along the way, you may uncover the nature of distraction and competition at different stages of the customer journey, and eventually be more purposeful and accurate with your sales pitch.

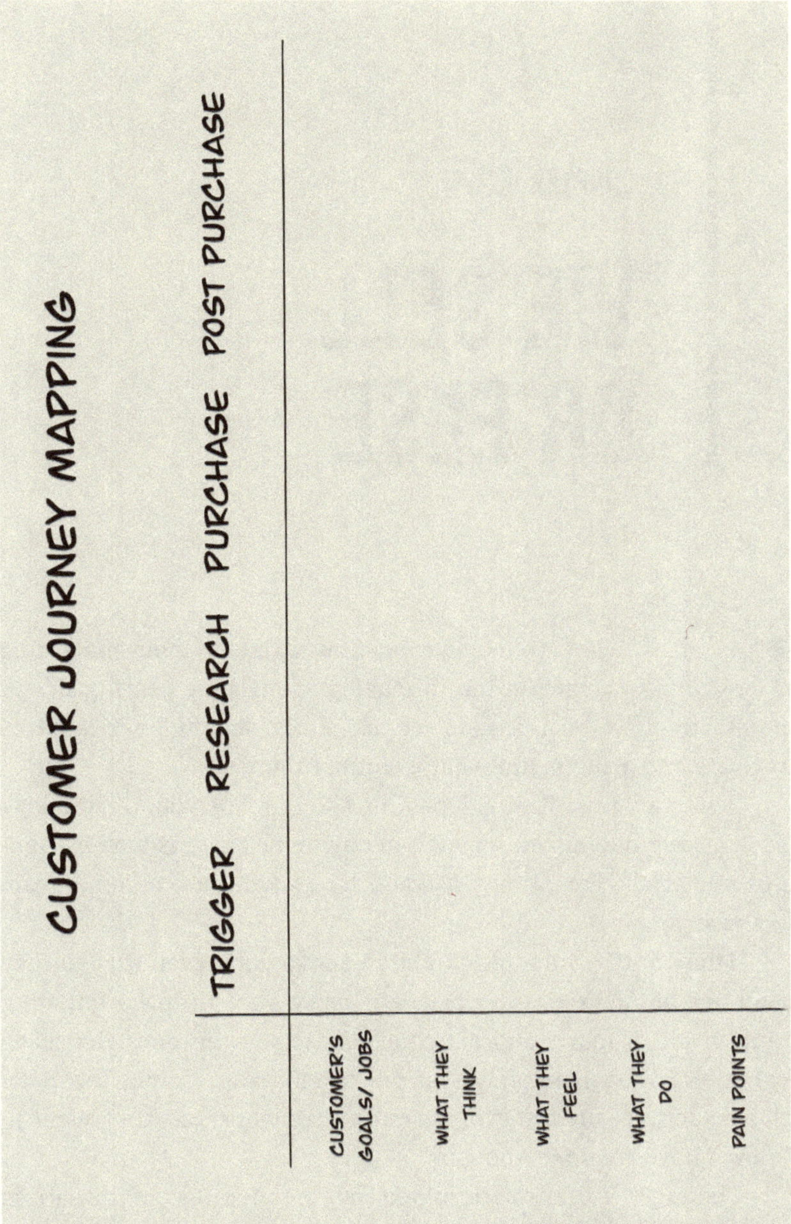

CUSTOMER JOURNEY MAPPING

TRIGGER   RESEARCH   PURCHASE   POST PURCHASE

CUSTOMER'S GOALS/ JOBS

WHAT THEY THINK

WHAT THEY FEEL

WHAT THEY DO

PAIN POINTS

Fig. 4.2: Use the Customer Journey Map framework to understand your customers.

CHAPTER 5

WE SELL OR ELSE

For many who are wondering how to start their marketing planning or whether they are doing enough, the bearing always points to their business objectives, these should be related to revenue and growth, not what is hot out there.

For start-ups, it could be the adoption of your technology such as app downloads, growth of customer base, as well as sign-ups and trials. For others, it could be growing the revenue from their customers.

Many of the start-up founders I spoke with, even though they may not be marketing trained, are savvy enough to be initiating quite a lot of marketing activities, especially the ones that have commercialised. Many, however, fall into the trap of doing too many things, and are unsure if they are on the right track, they want to know, "Have we done enough?"

"Enough" is not determined by the number of initiatives launched and there are no finite checklists.

Upon first identifying your target segment, it is likely that you would initially devote most of your resources to and experiment with every tactic possible to woo them. Over time, it is no longer sustainable to adopt the same approach with limited ammunition and companies must reprioritise those that showed traction in their earlier experiments. This is especially important for start-ups as they are most likely bootstrapped with limited resources and bandwidth.

One of the start-ups I mentored was planning to launch a series of dress watches that deliver good design and quality at an affordable price. They had done quite a bit of things on the branding and marketing front; their marketing tactics included the typical social media pages, webpage and paid ads. However, I was intrigued to discover that they had started a series of regular blogs and podcasts, their rationale for doing so was to inspire potential customer groups with advice and nuggets of wisdom from successful people.

While there is nothing wrong with podcasts and blogs, these are not the most pressing for this start-up at this nascent stage of its growth. Their priority should be to devote their limited resources to create demands for their watches. The podcasts could be considered at a later stage to enrich their brand experience and to engage their potential customers.

ALEXIS, BRIAN, AND CHLOE GO TO LUNCH

On a crowded street in the city centre at lunch time, Alexis got out of the cab and hastened her pace to the office. She had had a busy morning of multiple store visits for her work.

Next to the drop-off point, an appetising image of a cheeseburger beckoned. Alexis recalled that a new burger joint, Jones's Grub, had just opened around the corner. She looked at her phone and realised that only 10 minutes stood between her and the weekly conference call with the regional teams. She thought: It's lunchtime peak hour and there was no time for a sit-down lunch. It would be another two hours before she could do so. She decided that she would dash into Jones's Grub to order the featured set meal to go.

In an office nearby, Brian is almost done with his weekly sales report, and just needed to walk through a key account update from a fellow colleague, Brie. He decided to do this over lunch and scanned the food delivery app to order. There were quite a few food brands to choose from and Brian was in the mood for some hearty burgers.

A promotion from Jones's Grub popped up on the screen— they were offering free delivery and free sides for any order above $30. He asked his co-workers if they would be keen to join a group order. Some of them, having seen the brand being promoted by TikTok influencers, gladly agreed. Brian eventually placed an order for $40 and proceeded with his discussion with Brie while waiting for the food to be delivered to the office.

Meanwhile, Chloe arrived at the Jones's Grub bistro with her friend, Denise. They had not seen each for a few years, since graduating from college. Chloe had run into Denise two days ago and was thrilled to know that her friend now worked in the vicinity. Chloe had always loved the lunch set meals at Jones's Grub and carried their loyalty card. In addition, she also loved the dining ambience there. Hence, it was no surprise that Chloe would arrange to meet here for their long-due lunch.

Upon stepping into the bistro, the friends were quickly assigned a table. On the table was a tent card featuring the seasonal set meals for lunch and a special promotion of a free dessert for Jones's Grub loyalty card members.

We have just seen how different customers ended up eating at Jones's Grub Bistro.

With the exception of Chloe, whose choice to eat there was intentional, Brian landed on Jones's Grub during his search on the food delivery app and for Alexis, it was purely incidental. All three engaged with Jones's Grub at different proximities towards a successful sale with Jones's Grub. In other words, they are at different stages of a sales funnel. Jones's Grub's marketing team had created their funnel strategy to ensure they reached their prospects, win new customers, and also to encourage repeat purchases.

THE SALES FUNNEL

The funnel is also sometimes presented as the AIDA funnel (Fig. 5.1). AIDA refers to the buyers' states of mind as they progress through different stages of the buying journey.

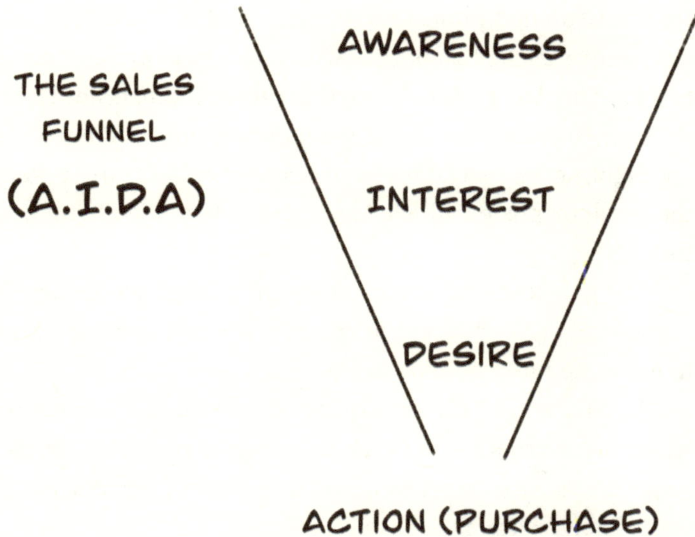

Fig. 5.1: The AIDA Sales Funnel.

A   stands for **awareness** of your brand or your category.

I   refers to **interest** in the benefits of your category and your product that encourage buyers to research more.

D   stands for **desires** for your products and services, especially when there is an emotional connection; the buyers like and want them.

A   is for **action** where buyers take the steps to engage, request for communications, or buy.

A sales funnel simply refers to
the journey potential customers go through
on their way to purchase.

Let's see how Jones's Grub worked their sales funnel:

- **A** and **I** correspond to the **top of the funnel (ToFU)**
  Jones's Grub had published the launch of the new store at the city centre such that both Alexis and Chloe are aware of its arrival. This could include anything from radio, branded video rolls on YouTube and social media platforms, influencer posts spotlighting its special menu as seen by Brian's co-workers, to the outdoor poster which Alexis saw when she alighted from the cab.

  The purposes of these communications are designed to place Jones's Grub brand at the top of consumers' minds and to generate interest in its menu.

  At this stage, the messages are designed for mediums where they are able to reach as many of their desired target segments as possible. The target audience may not actually be ready to make the purchase.

- **D** corresponds with the **middle of the funnel (MoFU)**
  Jones's Grub made sure that they stood out at the point where customers were choosing between different F&B (food and beverage) providers, such as when Brian was deciding what

to order for lunch. Brian might not be planning to order from Jones's Grub; he wasn't looking to satisfy any craving. The in-app notifications and featured ads made him notice Jones's Grub. What stood out for him could be the promotion, partly contributed by the tempting food imagery, or even the free delivery offer. Jones's Grub worked with the food delivery platform to feature the different kinds of stimuli to trigger a purchase desire.

- **A** corresponds with the **bottom of the funnel (BoFU)**
The desired actions take place here. It could include placing an order for your products, signing up for an event or course, booking a service, or even downloading your app. At this stage, you want your shopper to make the move to become your customer.

   This was where Brian was persuaded to upsize his order to qualify for the free delivery and free sides. This was also where Chloe decided to order the seasonal set meals and leverage her loyalty card for the free dessert. These were the final push factors for making the orders.

We can see from these references how Jones's Grub had designed their marketing funnels to ensure that they maximised the number of potential customers they could capture for acquisition.

It is highly possible that Alexis could have grabbed a takeaway lunch from the nearest place she passed on the way to her office had she not seen the outdoor poster. Likewise, Brian could have ordered from any food brands on his food delivery app. Jones's Grub had started cultivating a following from Chloe by selling her their loyalty card, which motivated her to dine with them again.

Beyond the food preferences and quality, I believe Jones's Grub also worked to deliver an appealing dining experience that builds the love for its brand.

As the term suggests, the funnel is an inverted triangle that is broader at the top of the funnel and tapers towards the bottom. These stages do vary according to the nature of the business.

Deploying the right marketing resources and investment at different stages of the funnel will be key to the success of your marketing strategy and whether you are able to meet your marketing objectives, whether it's for awareness, new customer acquisition, customer retention, or advocacy.

For your marketing tactics to be effective, you would need to demonstrate how you can make customers' decision-making easier and friction-free. For example, the in-app promotions helped Brian justify making a bigger order.

There are other frameworks like flywheel and growth loops that are said to replace the funnel framework, we will talk about how they are all, in principle, aligned, in chapter 7.

THE VALUE CONE

When Jones's Grub closed the sales with Alexis, Brian, and Chloe and many others like them, they successfully transformed buying intent into revenue.

Most marketing textbooks suggest that it can cost five times more than retaining an existing customer. Five, as a factor, really depends on the category and your time in the market, but it certainly would cost more to win a new customer.

Chloe, for example, is a returning customer of Jones's Grub. Jones's Grub might have spent money to entice her to make her first purchase and to sign up for their loyalty programme. Her subsequent visits to Jones's Grub became more intentional. Jones's Grub would want to have more orders for returning customers like Chloe.

Now they could do the same with Alexis and Brian, and offer them an incentive for a second order. They could also invite them to join its loyalty programme, like its Facebook page, or be on the promotion update email list.

Your customers probably navigated hurdles of complex purchase decision-making and buying journeys to eventually land on you. It only makes sense to want to maximise the mileage of your marketing dollars by enticing these new customers to come back and buy from you again, or renew service contracts.

Just imagine, when every one of your existing customers come back to buy from you again, you would have just doubled your sales.

By continuing to deliver great customer experience through its food and services, Jones's Grub had created a fan in Chloe, who chose to dine at Jones's Grub again, and bring her friend Denise. In convincing Denise to eat at Jones's Grub, she might potentially have bragged about the food joint and her past dining experience.

As the potential customers move through the sales funnel towards the point of sales conversion, the path to growth exists in the form of a value cone. Thereafter, you should look into building a continuous momentum for growth, which we will touch on in chapter 7.

Essentially, the value cone (Fig. 5.2, overleaf) is an upright funnel that extends from the point of purchase. It comprises three portions:

- Repeat;
- Loyalty; and
- Advocacy.

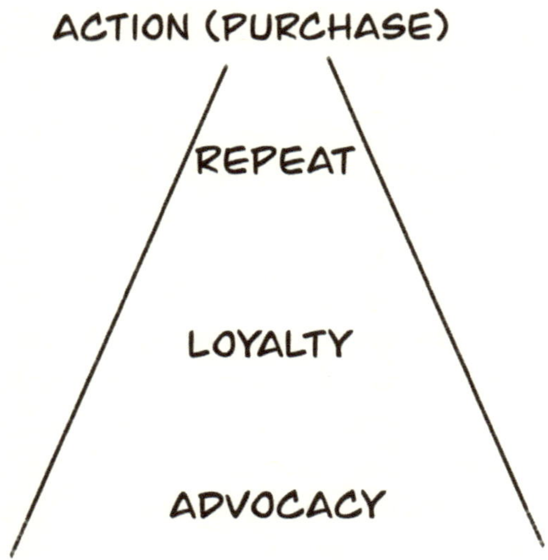

Fig. 5.2: The Value Cone.

A number of elements are at work in the value cone, beyond the incentive and programme designed to cultivate loyalty. True brand loyalty happens when the customers establish emotional connections with your brand, trust your products, feel satisfied with your service such that they make your brand their preference.

Customers will choose to patronise Jones's Grub again because it makes their life easier—it's easier to dine in or order from a place that is perceived to give them value for money, good food, and a great place to hang out.

Over time, when these loyal customers become believers in your product and start recommending you to their family and friends, they are now your advocates and helping you to attract more customers.

Now, assuming you have the same marketing budget to deploy on the same tactics for acquisitions, while at the same time your value cone is working, there will be a potential upside to your revenue.

Conversely, if your sales target remains the same and you already enjoy steady traction from returning customers, you would end up reducing your reliance on paid marketing.

Let's look at another example in an industry that we are familiar with—airlines.

Attractive fares, extensive routes, and good reviews for in-flight features and services are just some of the many reasons for people picking the airlines they want to fly with. Frequent flyer miles programmes are the main reasons drawing people back to fly with a particular airline.

I love flying Singapore Airlines not because it is my national airline, but because it continues to deliver one of the best flying experiences and has been decorated over the years with awards such as World's Best Airline Cabin Staff, Best Airline in Asia, Best Economy Class Onboard Catering, etc. In addition, I feel at home and safe flying Singapore Airlines because I find it reliable and efficient—I have an emotional connection with the brand.

I also like the fact that it's part of the Star Alliance with many established airlines as its members, which means that I can earn miles which can in turn be converted as KrisFlyer points, to be redeemed for flights on Singapore Airlines.

Having said that, there are still airlines within the Star Alliance which I would not touch from a million miles—I arrived at my decisions by reading airline reviews from critics and real customers.

This is a good example that reward programmes do not guarantee true loyalty unless you get your basic service standard and product efficacy right.

AN EFFECTIVE VALUE CONE

Here are some checklists to guide you towards building your customer base and growing the value per customer.

1   Channel for Continual Communication and Engagement
  * Do you provide at least one channel for feedback and post-sales communications?
  * Do you gather customers' feedback to understand what the customers/client like and don't like about your products or services?
  * Do you have a plan for service recovery?

2   Repeat Purchase
  * Do you have an incentive for customers to have another sale with you in the near future?
  * Do you have complimentary products or services you can invite your customers to try?
  * Do you have a channel to serve up future notifications for promotions and deals?

3   Loyalty
  * Do you reward points to customers for buying from you?
  * Do you provide preferential services or perks for customers to spend more money with you over time?
  * Do you find ways to continue to support them on the use of your services and products?
  * Do you add value to their usage experience?

4   Advocacy
- Do you reward your customers for showing off your brands?
- Do you make it easy for customers to recommend you?

CHAPTER 6

THE NET, THE HOOK, AND THE CHAOTIC MIDDLE GROUND

In the early 2000s, I chanced upon the movie *Big Shot's Funeral* whose plot revolved around a world-renowned American film director (Tyler) who was shooting a remake of *The Last Emperor* in Beijing. His ailing health caused him to be booted from his job and he eventually suffered a stroke and fell into a coma. His assistant hired a down-and-out man (YoYo) to plan a comedy funeral inspired by the traditional Chinese funeral for the elderly.

YoYo then discovered that Tyler is literally bankrupt and therefore had no money to pay for anything. YoYo had to enlist the help of a businessman friend to get as many sponsors as the funeral process would allow. The result was a hilarious showcase of product placements and corporate sponsorships. The "dead" was adorned with a mobile phone, soft drinks, sports shoes, drinking water, accessories, apparel, etc. There were even giant billboards and blow-up ads at the funeral venue.

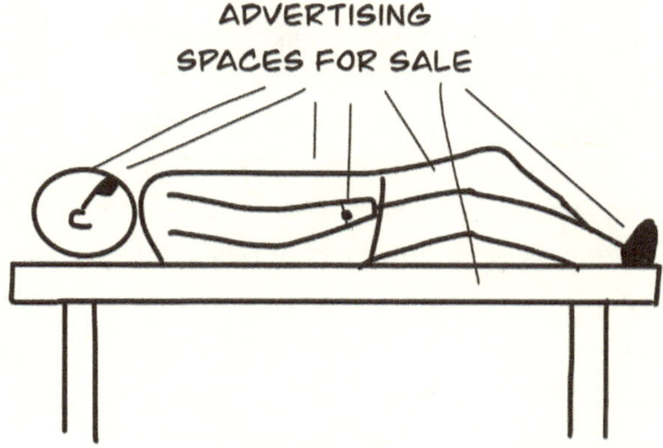

Fig. 6.1: Parody of soft advertisements practices.

This dark comedy presents a parody of soft advertisements practice (Fig. 6.1) in the film industry that is still prevalent in the current day. Scriptwriters are fed lists of paid sponsors to be incorporated into the setting and story lines, these incidental brand spot lights adulterate seemingly good plots especially when some are deliberately scripted.

Brands that are planted in most TV dramas range from online gaming accessories, furniture, face masks, beauty products, medicine, beverages, automobiles, snacks ... the list goes on. Having been in the creative industry and personally been involved in incidental product placement, I can spot these implants quickly.

Even Hollywood films with big production budgets adopt similar tactics. James Bond movies, for example, are popular platforms to showcase the hot wheels of their times. Sunbeam Alpine, Bentley Mark, Aston Martin, Ford Mustang, AMC Hornet, Mercury Cougar, Audi, BMW, and even Toyota 2000 GT are among the fleet driven by 007.

Many brands go into these platforms believing that it enables the audience to develop strong connections in a more natural way rather than being directly marketed to. As viewers, we become aware of them, talk about them, and search for them online.

I am, by no means, advocating paid product placements as these can be expensive outlays.

Product placement plays to the principle of capturing the target audience at the point when they are not looking for you. Because they are not attacked by aggressive sales pitch, they are likely to be more open-minded to appraise your product, and even enjoy being subtly "sold to".

Doing it well, of course, is another story. I am sad to say some need better finesse.

CASTING THE NET AT THE TOP OF THE FUNNEL

In the beginning, your potential customers may not have heard about you and are, therefore, unfamiliar with you. When your business is new, your priority is getting your name out there to prospects who would be your first customers. However, they may not be actively looking for your solutions.

I have personally been on the receiving end of countless attempts where suppliers would reach me via LinkedIn or cold emails to pitch their services to my organisation. They all request that I part with 15–30 minutes of my time to find out about their services.

Most of the time I would have absolutely no interest to respond unless they are able to do this:

- Be seen as a thought leader in their category or the subject of their domain, and be a brand I have the opportunity to see before at webinars or at conferences;
- Demonstrate that they understand what my organisation's challenges are;
- Show me valuable insights and study about my industry; and
- Clearly articulate their potential value proposition and make it practical, not conceptual.

In the same way, your prospects would pay you attention if you show that you are more knowledgeable and able to add value. No one is willing to spend time telling you about their business, they want to hear you talk about their business, as well as share useful information and knowledge.

Ultimately, you need to entice them to start a conversation with you.

> ## Put yourselves in front of the potential customer segment
> ## with needs you can address.

Let's take a leaf from professional fishermen who know where to cast their nets for the best catch. They studied the behaviour of the target catch (fish) to predict where they're likely to be, given a specific area, time of year, and set of weather and water conditions. They keep detailed logs with weather conditions, temperatures, dates, coordinates and other notes about their catches.

In the earlier chapter, we touched on the different ways to enrich our understanding of the target segment that will improve our precision on where we should be casting our net. The following are some common tactics at the top of the funnel.

Product Placement

The brands who chose product placement in films hope to ride on the potential eyeballs the sponsored films would garner. The scenario where the product is featured provides the context of how it's used, who uses it, the usage occasion, product experience, and in some cases, associated prestige.

Product placements can also be done on a smaller scale. For example, I have seen branded hairdryers being installed in the changing room of fitness centres to be used by its patrons, with a decal placed on the changing room mirror stating that the hairdryers are being sponsored by the brand, along with an offer that can be redeemed at the reception.

Mass Paid Brand Advertising

Mass paid brand advertising on offline media like press, television, and even those that are outdoor are the conventional modes of top of the funnel channels. These are usually more costly and there are potentially high wastages as the majority of its audience are too far from making any purchase decisions.

Sponsored product placements and offline mass advertising may not be ideal for businesses with limited budgets. Instead, they should be more selective about the channels and focus on generating interest, building awareness, educating and establishing credentials among the desired target segment, not everybody.

Share Your Brand Stories

Tell your brand stories on your website, LinkedIn page, and social media platforms. These would be branded content such as the "WHY" behind your business, evidence of how you are able to bring success to your clients, how you appreciate and empathise with the challenges of your potential customers, and other content that build trust and confidence. And if you are a me-too in your category, your brand stories should address how you are different. Branded content that add value to potential customers can earn voluntary time spent with the brand and eventually own a space in their hearts and minds.

Often, companies design their website for transactions. It is important to cater to different groups of visitors. Other than customers and shoppers, there could also be accidental browsers and explorers who are trying to size you up but not looking to make a booking with you.

Customer testimonials and past media coverage are other great ways to be featured on your owned channels.

Pitch Your Story to the Media

Bill Gates of Microsoft had this quote which sums up the importance of PR: "If I was down to my last dollar, I would spend it on PR."

Good PR efforts are essential to help your company shape a positive public image and enhance reputation. They can help you attract potential investors, strategic partners, and talents for hire.

Conventional PR practices advocate cultivating relationships with the key media and engage the journalists for informal coffee chats, introducing them to your CEOs and founders. Good rapport with the media can come in handy when you want to share an inside story, exclusive scoops, or even future crisis communication.

Remember that the press is inundated with requests and pitches by organisations to tell their stories. Here are some ways to stand out for the story to be picked up:

1   **Newsjacking of current conversations also presents opportunities to develop newsworthy stories**

    Madame Tussauds Wax Museum made the news by removing Prince Harry and Meghan Markle from a wax display of the British Royal Family, shortly after they announced their decision to step down as senior members of the Family. The move by the wax museum enabled them to gain publicity and viral attention, by riding on the news of upheaval among the Royals.

    In 2019, there was a buzz in social media about a bizarre plan to "Storm Area 51". Area 51 had long been theorised to host testing extraterrestrials. Oreo joked on its Twitter feed: "What flavours do you think they are hiding in #Area51?". This was followed by reshares and responses by thousands of users and even other brands. Oreo instantly gets people to discuss its great flavours.

    However, caution needs to be taken with any newsjacking attempts by considering if the strategy is tasteful or offensive.

In the wake of the tragic Boston Marathon bombing in 2013, Epicurious, an online food publication tweeted: "In honour of Boston and New England, may we suggest: wholegrain cranberry scones" with attached links to a recipe. This was followed by: "Boston: Our hearts are with you. Here's a bowl of breakfast energy we could all use to start today", also with attached links to a recipe.

Tweeting breakfast treats and attempting to promote their own content in response to a tragic event where people were killed is not only insensitive but also distasteful. The brand was eventually forced to apologise.

2 **Creative original stories**

A four-foot-high statue of a defiant girl was erected across the charging bull statue on Wall Street in New York on the morning of International Women's Day in 2017. This was commissioned by investment management firm State Street Global Advisors as part of their campaign towards more women representations on the board. By standing up to the Charging Bull, she is standing up for gender diversity. The publicity stunt was a powerful expression of a strong message that is more vivid than a press release, and it is original.

In 2014, the Ice Bucket Challenge took the world by storm with videos of personalities and ordinary people dumping a bucket of ice water over their heads. This started off as a stunt to raise awareness of ALS or Lou Gehrig's disease, which is a neurodegenerative disease.

I was among the millions of people who were challenged to dump ice water over their heads to experience a brief moment of brain freeze and subsequently challenged others to follow suit. This viral challenge to get people to experience brain freeze raised more than $115 million dollars, where most of the funding went to the ALS Association and research on the disease.

3   **Impressionable media drops and influencer packages**
Remember the trays of eggs that were delivered by Air Canada to the travel agents? That was actually an interesting way to capture the attention of its recipient.

In the present day, the same present of interesting optics are applied in many packages that are sent to the press and influencers. They work like a 3D press release in Instagram-worthy packaging.

These packages pack in branded elements to provide a tangible product experience at home accompanied by talking points on the brand. It can include a personalised note and sometimes a complimentary gift.

The end goal for these packages is to get picked up by the press, and for the influencers to share about it via social media. For the latter, it is common to find social media handles, suggested hashtags, and even a promo code for their followers.

Deliver Insights and Thought Leadership Conversations

I participated in an interesting panel discussion organised by Oracle that was titled, "Marketing in a Cookie-constrained World". The panel raised the questions of whether digital marketing has hit a dead-end with increasing restrictions on marketing tracking cookies.

The marketers who attended the webinar panel wanted to understand how they could circumvent this development. While the panellists deliberated on their respective efforts on building profile-able data, Oracle's representative on the panel spoke about their new suite of solutions that would do just that and improve audience intelligence. This is essentially a sales pitch but padded with insight exchanges among experienced marketers, in a non-threatening platform.

By orchestrating the webinar to discuss subject matter its target segment is highly concerned about, Oracle established themselves as thought leaders who not only provided useful insights and perspectives, but potentially the solutions as well.

Conference speaking appearances is a popular channel used by B2B solution and service providers to improve exposure to their brands. Brands should select conferences with the desired audience profile and curate their messages to align with the theme of the conference. Make these informative, educational, and thought-provoking, as most conference organisers discourage heavy sales pitches and are often the ones to set the topics.

Search Engine Optimisation

Search Engine Optimisation, also referred to as SEO, can come across as complex and intimidating. It is essentially allowing your brand to be searchable and discoverable.

When SEO is done well, your brand might be among the first listings when people search for words or subjects related to your business offering, or problems they are trying to solve.

There are a number of best practices to adopt such as:

- Publish quality content such as published blogs, white papers with relevant keywords, on blogs, websites, social media pages, and even your app store descriptions;
- Curate keywords and phrases in your metadata for web page titles, descriptions and even long-tail keyword phrases;
- Update content regularly; and
- Get backlinks to your site from authoritative and credible sites.

It helps to engage a specialist to fix this at the initial stage until you have built your own team.

Community Marketing

In the book, *Tractions*, authors Gabriel Weinberg and Justin Mares share in detail how 19 channels can be used to help companies build traction across the different stages of the sales funnels. Other than what we have just covered, trade shows, speaking engagements, and community building are also other channels worth activating at the top of the channel.

For example, a business hoping to attract a specific traveller segment may either infiltrate a travel forum by planting brand ambassadors there to participate in the conversations and "promote" or "recommend" the brand as the conversation leads.

In 2014, insurance company, Income, started an Instagram handle titled "Travel Made Yours" that invited travellers to post their "spots hidden and roads less ridden" travel photos to aggregate user-generated contents featuring travel recommendations and useful travel tips. By helping travellers and celebrating unique experiences, Income is well placed to build affinity among their desired target segment and potentially in travellers' mental shopping list.

THE CHAOTIC PATH TO PURCHASE

Getting my daughter into a good primary school in Singapore was probably one of the most daunting journeys I had to endure as a parent. Like any typical Asian parent who wants their children to grow up as successful doctors and lawyers, the tiger mom traits that run in my blood meant that I wanted the best for my only child too.

Many Singaporean parents would resort to doing community work for the school precinct and volunteering for the school of their choice as early as two years in advance; others would even purchase or rent expensive properties to secure an address in close proximity to the desired school vicinity, so as to qualify for earlier phases of registration.

By the time I had discovered these, I was already late to the game compared to my well-prepared peers. With only less than three months to go before the day of registration, I realised that the school of my choice was out of reach. As such, I had to scout around frantically for information.

The go-to place for this matter of life and death was the site KiasuParents.com. *Kiasu* is a Singapore slang in Chinese dialect which means "fear of losing out".

KiasuParents.com presents parents of school-going kids with a treasure trove of information on the phases and procedures related to school admissions. It has analysis of the past year's application and balloting chances, individual school reviews more comprehensive than those published on the Singapore Ministry of Education website.

There were also tracks of discussions in the forum for all possible issues and topics related to the kids starting their education journey. Parents were the ones giving advice to other parents. In addition, I was speaking with friends who had gone through the ordeal as well as advice from strangers over social media.

For the primary schools, getting students was not an issue for them; after all, education for Singaporean kids is highly subsidised by the government. The panic belongs to the parents. And I was right at the epicentre of panic—I had the intent and had admitted my problems, and was then evaluating options for the best possible decision and courses of action.

Twelve years on and we are back on the search, but this time, looking at overseas universities where she would pursue her degree. Most universities provide subsidised education for their domestic students in the host countries but reap the revenue from international students who pay full fees.

No effort is spared to court potential students. Not only do the universities work with external admission consultants to serve and sell to prospective students, they provide customised admission guides on how specific polytechnic graduates could transfer in. There are also plenty of videos and content online on accommodation, student lives, and virtual tours.

Engagement, information, and education take on the main tune. This is where brands should establish engagement and trust-based relationships with leads. At this stage, the goal is to unobtrusively make people buy. The middle funnel is probably one of the most dynamic battlefields of mind for needs, wants, and choices. This is where consumers can get derailed on their way to sealing the deal.

We know for a fact that the path to purchase is not linear and the most dynamic part lies in the middle funnel. This is where a brand should demonstrate its value proposition.

Stand Out at the Point of Sales

In 2005, Procter and Gamble (P&G) coined the term, "First Moment of Truth (FMOT) to refer to the moment when the customer chooses a product over the other competitors' offerings. It suggests that there is a window of 3–5 seconds during which the consumer encounters the product and the time with which the marketer is able to turn the shoppers into buyers. While the context in which P&G built this is for the dynamic of an in-store merchandising environment, the dilemma and dynamics of decision making is true for the middle of the funnel.

The retail store is, by far, the most visible illustration of the middle funnel in action, with the average number of product assortments in a supermarket ranging between 15,000 to 60,000, product packaging, merchandising, product placement on shelves are all levers to pull in order to break the visual clutter at the point of sales.

However, the "point of sales" can exist in many forms. It might be on the e-commerce marketplace or social media platforms, and even the YouTube menu.

Win the Mind Game

Competition may not be confined within concentrated spaces like retail outlets; some battlegrounds are on strategic keywords and search pages. Keyword bidding is when competing brands spend to dominate keywords in Google Ads, in order to gain a more favourable ranking in search results. There can be multiple keywords in ad groups and investing in multiple ad groups can be an expensive affair.

Blog posts, white papers, web or in-app pop ups, email campaigns, FAQs, case studies, and webinars, can be used by brands to:

- Relate to potential buyers' needs to the products features and attributes;
- Engage and gauge prospects' readiness to buy; and
- Raise confidence to move people closer to buy.

The middle ground for B2B businesses is where leads generated at the top of the funnel are handed over to follow-through by dedicated sales efforts. Limited-time offers, product trial campaigns, no-obligation consultation and assessments are often deployed to close in on the sales.

Strategic Partnership to Gain a Head Start

Sometimes the best way to gain entry into a new market segment is to tap onto the established network of strategic partners to access immediate customer segments and joint marketing resources, collaborating to multiply the impact of their sales efforts.

For example, a new telehealth service provider can work with established insurance administrators to gain credibility which would otherwise take longer to build on their own. They can also have immediate access to a ready pool of potential patients who are referred from the strategic partner's insured base.

They may also collaborate with travel booking platforms to offer remote travel related medical checks to ready pools of travellers.

Address the "No"

There are many reasons potential customers would say "no" or "not now" at the critical point of closing a sale. These can include:

- "I still do not get it"

  Potential customers might still fail to understand your product. They do not find it relevant for them and do not see how it meets their needs.

  Maybe there was too much information to absorb during the sales pitch phase. In cases like this, it would help to summarise the key reasons to buy and get them to say "yes" to each and every one, as well as provide context on how the product can be used, e.g., product sampling, proof of concept, and past use cases.

- "Do not know how to make this work"

  Potential customers might have already been sold on the benefits but they are not sure how to integrate your product into their current operation process. They might need to involve other parties or stakeholders to make this work.

  It helps to understand who the key players are in the implementation of the product and try to invite them into your sales pitch earlier. For example, a retail tech company selling smart shopping carts to a retailer would need to address not just the retail operation team, they would need to answer queries from the retailer's IT team on how the sensors could be set up in-store and potential bandwidth for signal transmission. They might also involve the marketing team to demonstrate potential user scenarios for contents that can be served by the cart.

It would be great to share examples of how it has been successfully implemented in other similar customers, and show that the prospect's potential challenges can be addressed. If you are pitching to your first customer and do not have the benefit of a proven case study, showing that you thought about their potential challenges would help.

- "I see risk"
  This can apply to new technology perceived as disruptive, new business models that require a shift in the paradigm, or even new entrants into an existing category where there are already more established incumbents.

In these scenarios, it would help to highlight similarities of your products compared to what the prospects are familiar with, and then explain how your product is differentiated and better.

Here's an example. Years ago, my company was tasked to help a financial institution launch a (then) low-risk investment product targeted at saving and fixed deposit customers. The client had discovered that a big group of their customers kept their money in savings and fixed deposits accounts, which are considered liabilities for banks.

The client created an investment product which worked like a unit trust or mutual fund but was structured to retain the investment capital. However, most of these customers were risk averse and would stay away from anything remotely called a mutual fund.

We managed to successfully launch this and ended up breaking the client's sales target by doing the following:

- We highlighted the similarities between this product and the more familiar deposit products, that the capital is guaranteed and protected. That helped to address most of the fear of venturing into new financial products.

- We pitched on the benefit that "the only way is UP". Even though the potential upsides in return could be marginally unpredictable compared to the fixed interest earning, customers lapped up the hope of the potential upside.
- The product was not named as a fund even though it came with a prospectus that accompanied most mutual funds. We chose a name that was approachable—it was called "UP" and the key visual of the product featured an adorable dog with long ears pointing skyward, defying gravity.
- The communications were kept simple and easy to understand. It was a breath of fresh air compared to the serious and boring advertisements on mutual funds, and this helped us to clearly differentiate the new investment product.

THE HOOK TO TURN SHOPPERS INTO CUSTOMERS

I once had to stock up the pantry before a work trip. After browsing an online grocer for an hour and accumulating a sizeable cart for checkout, I discovered that there was no way for me to receive my supply before leaving for my trip due to the lack of delivery slots. Frustrated and disappointed, I decided to abandon my cart and went shopping at a competitor's platform instead.

As I had similar futile shopping experiences with the same grocer previously, that incident was the last straw that broke the camel's back—that grocer lost me as a customer. It would be quite a while before I would shop with them again.

I wonder if the original online grocer had tracked the size and the quantity of past abandoned carts as well as bounce at the checkout page, they could easily calibrate the loss of potential sales. These statistics would justify them improving the delivery fulfilment support.

After generating awareness and interest prospects at the top of the funnel, engaging, persuading, and building confidence at the middle funnel, the ultimate goal of this courtship dance is to bring the leads to the point of "commitment", where the shoppers finally cash the cheque for the value you had promised to deliver and become your customer.

This is the critical point of the purchase journey where brands make it easy and friction-free for shoppers to close that sale.

Powerful calls to action, attractive
incentives, payment options,
fulfilment services, customer service, and
responsiveness to enquiries
all play a role in increasing an urgency to
close the sales.

Customer Experience and Customer Service Can Make or Break the Sale

We were once commissioned by a ferry operator to help them identify and improve conversions for ticket bookings. During our usability tests, we recruited potential customers as testers who were asked to book tickets online based on a few user scenarios, catering to different family profiles and needs.

Every reaction, emotion, and action observed throughout each of the booking sessions was recorded and probed. Our user experience researcher queried the testers on their motivations as well as frustrations behind each action.

For example, we observed that people wanted to see, in real time, how the total cost of their fare would change as they choose different timings and different time bands. They wanted to be prompted proactively for any discounts which were applicable. Other gaps observed would include payment options and navigation challenges.

The findings were consolidated and fed to the client's engineering team who would eventually refine the user interface for the booking site. This would be a vital part of their continuous improvement as they monitored abandoned carts and grew good reviews.

When I started buying shoes and apparel online, there were always concerns about getting the right fit. Not being able to try out the outfit to see how it fits on the body but only relying on size charts provided became a barrier for many potential shoppers. It didn't help that the size M varies according to different fashion labels.

When I bought my first pair of shoes online on Zalora, I decided to test out the size chart by ordering a cheaper pair of flats, in two sizes. Zalora had a fuss-free return policy which allowed me to return my purchase at no cost.

My package arrived a few days later, with a resealable bag and a form for potential returns. And the return was easy! I simply had to put the wrong-sized shoes into the return bag, with the form stating the reason for return. Thereafter, I could just drop off the return package at the post office near my house. I was pleasantly surprised to discover there was a designated counter at the post offices to receive the return package with no additional form-filling or questions asked.

This experience paved the way for many future purchases of shoes. It also helped that Zalora had a customer service hotline with someone who actually answered calls and sounded eager to address all my queries about returns.

I become an advocate for the brand.

Entice to Close

What are different ways to sell a shirt, a pair of pants, and a pair of sunglasses for $60?

We can construct the offer these ways:

- **Option 1:** Shirt + Pants for $60, and get a pair of sunglasses for free

The gift with purchase tactic gives customers the satisfaction of enjoying freebies and getting more for the value they pay.

- **Option 2:** Shirt + Pants for $60, and get a pair of sunglasses for free when you buy within the promotion period
Limited promotion period tactic creates a sense of scarcity and drives urgency for purchase.
- **Option 3:** Shirt + Pants for $60, and get a pair of sunglasses. You can pay in two instalments.
Instalments work especially well for bigger price tags and reduce the pain of upfront cash outlay.
- **Option 4:** Buy 2 sets of shirts and pants for less than $120.
This tactic encourages customers to trade up for bigger cart purchases and halves your efforts in driving incremental sales.

Companies offering services, SaaS, and B2B subscription services often adopt freemium to encourage trials and reduce barriers to buy. However, there must always be a plan to convert free trial users into paying customers.

Here are some ways to do so:
- Make your products or service easy to use;
- Keep the free trials to basic version of your products and upsell the more premium features (increased functionality and user licence);
- Train your user to achieve quick wins through your products;
- Conduct regular performance reviews of client's success to reinforce your value proposition (e.g., business success);
- Create a sense of urgency with an offer that expires within a limited time frame; and
- Schedule a call or meeting, or even a discount near the end of the free trial to encourage sales.

There is typically a long sales cycle for enterprise products that involve more decision makers. It would help to support the potential clients in their internal sell-through by offering to prepare the presentations and materials needed for management approvals.

In summary, always make it attractive,
easy, and safe for your customer
to seal the deal with you.

Abandoned Carts and Dropped Calls are Not Lost Causes

Behind every abandoned cart lies the efforts of a potential customer who is open to do business with you. Some online retailers did well to re-target those unchecked carts with an offer to seal the deal. Likewise, if bookings are done through calls, swift follow-ups on dropped calls will ensure that your efforts at the top of the funnel are not wasted.

CLASSROOM

TRUMPING THE "NO"

- Outline the possible reasons your potential customers might say "no" to you.
- Craft a response or tactic to circumvent the reasons that you have just come up with.
- Now, improve your pitch at the top and middle part of the funnel by incorporating the ideas presented in this chapter.

CHAPTER 7

GROWTH ENGINE

G rowth is absolutely essential to the survival of business. A growing and financially stable company can amass more resources to pursue new business opportunities and develop more comprehensive offerings towards their bigger vision. A high growth company evokes confidence and is better at attracting the best talents.

Growth can manifest in different dimensions.

In an earlier chapter, we touched on growth in terms of growing the value per customer with the value cone, by driving repeat purchase and growing the pool of loyal returning customers.

Common tactics for driving repeat purchase include incentive programmes, vouchers for repeat purchases, as well as rewards programmes that accumulate points by enticing you to keep buying. Almost everyone—including theme parks, retailers, airlines, and F&B outlets—practise this legitimate "bribery". These structured rewards and loyalty programmes can take a bit of effort to set up and they can be potentially costly to maintain.

Real loyalty needs to work on the sensory and emotional levels, starting with product efficacy and service experience.

GETTING THE DUCKS IN A ROW

As the saying goes, no amount of advertising can sell a bad product. Likewise, no amount of loyalty programmes and rewards incentives can salvage bad product performance or below par services.

Take dining at a restaurant as an example. If you had a meal where cold food was served by an arrogant service crew, would you patronise the restaurant even if you are offered incentives to dine there again?

As such, before we jump at the marketing team for not delivering repeat visits, sometimes we might want to check that our product is working and we have services that delight customers.

Sometimes the best clues for fixing product performance and service delivery can be found in customer reviews and feedback. The importance of keeping a finger on the pulse of what the customers think goes beyond gathering insights for improvements. It also needs to capture negative reviews for service recovery as many could be posted on the public platforms.

AFTER SALES SUPPORT

Go beyond selling products by lending support to help your customers achieve success—show them that you are going above and beyond to help them. Successful companies build strong after-sales support to deliver higher customer satisfaction, brand loyalty, and customer advocacy. Warranty services, instruction manuals, library of contents on usage, fixes, and how-to guides are just some examples.

After sales support for B2B services focus on building business success for their clients, with dedicated account managers, regular business reviews, and consulting services.

Software developer HubSpot, for example, deploys activation consultants to train their clients' team on how to set up their instances on its platforms, and then hand-hold them to explore and trial more features offered on the platform. As their client starts to use their software more and integrate this into their business operations, it becomes easier to convince them to renew subscriptions for their software and potentially upsell for upgrades to more premium plans.

DELIVER BLISS

Have you read the story of the Fisherman by German writer Heinrich Boll?

It relates that a fisherman, while relaxing on a beautiful beach with his fishing rod, had an encounter with a businessman. The businessman asked the fisherman why he wasn't working harder to make a living for himself and his family by catching more fish, instead of lying on the beach.

Fisherman asked what would catching more fish bring him, to which the businessman replied, "To buy bigger nets for catching more fish", then "buy a boat to catch more fish" and "eventually own a fleet of fishing boats, hire help to work for him".

"What would my reward be?" the fisherman asked.

And the business replied, "You can be so rich that you never have to work for a living again. You can spend the rest of your days sitting on the beach, looking at the sunset and not have any care in the world!"

The fisherman smiled, looked up and said "And what do you think I am doing right now?"

Everyone has different definitions of what brings happiness. To many, success is related to making lots of money.

I believe that as we embark on the same question-and-answer drill, we will find ourselves back to the basic universal human needs of what makes happiness.

Here are some of them:

- Physical health and mental well-being;
- Food and water;
- Safety and security;
- Structure and control;
- Belongingness;
- Love and respect from others;
- Self-esteem; and
- Purpose to stay alive.

Among the common regrets that people have at the end of life, many wish to be more loving, spend more time with family, take more risks, pursue their dream, take care of health, and live a more meaningful life.

If we are able to pluck the right heartstrings with our customers, we will win loyalty and advocacy at an emotional level.

KNOW YOUR CUSTOMERS

Among your customers' data is a treasure trove waiting to be unearthed. Most early-stage start-ups may not have sufficient data points in their business to generate comprehensive insights. Nevertheless, here are some of the things you can start looking out for:

- How frequent and how recent your customer bought from you, and the monetary value of their orders;
- What they bought; and
- When they stopped buying from you.

These data are useful for understanding customers' preference on how to cross-sell complementary products and to encourage existing customers to spend more in future purchases. For example, someone who had previously bought a necklace and pendant set could be sold matching earrings, bracelets, and even interchangeable pendants.

Understanding the pattern of returning orders enables us to know when is the best time to trigger repeat orders. For example, the times to renew paid memberships or magazine subscriptions are predictable, as are the estimated length of usage time for products such as diapers, etc.

Newton's Cradle Momentum

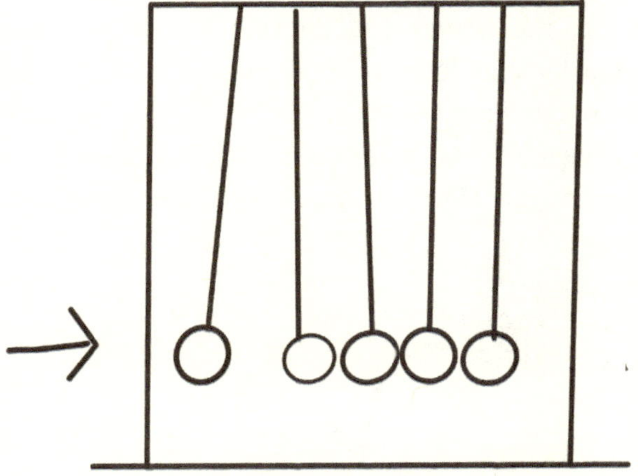

Fig. 7.1: Newton's Cradle.

Newton's Cradle (Fig. 7.1) is a device where five metal balls are suspended from a frame by thin wires, positioned just barely touching one another. When the ball at one end of the cradle is pulled away from the others and then released, it strikes the next ball and the remaining stationary balls and sends force through all of them to push the ball on the other end away.

The last ball then swings back and strikes the rest of the balls, repeating the movement in a steady rhythm. Apparently, this continuous momentum could last up to three to five years with proper care!

Every business needs to think about how they can ride on a continuous momentum to drive continuous growth. This is especially true for start-ups without deep pockets.

A well-curated sales funnel that is diligently manicured for efficiency works like the first ball in Newton's Cradle that sets off an unstoppable chain reaction. However, frameworks like Flywheel and Growth Loops are said to replace the funnel framework.

THE FLYWHEEL AND THE LOOP

HubSpot uses the Flywheel model to advocate the importance of building loyalty and love by delivering remarkable experiences around customer success.

The Flywheel has three continuous trines in continuous momentum: Attract Shopper, Engage Prospect, Delight Customer.

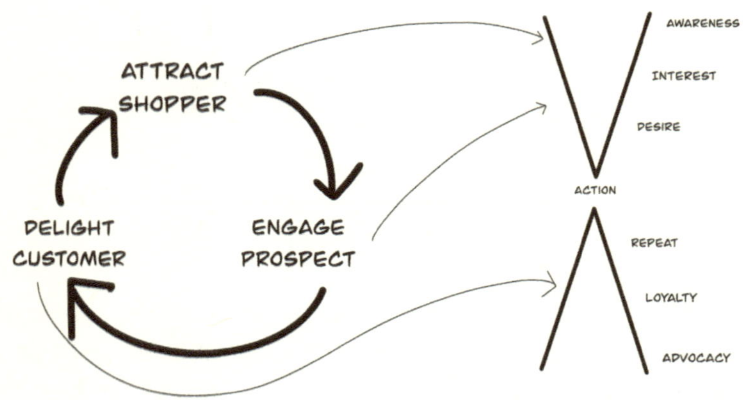

Fig. 7.2: The Flywheel.

The delighted customers who become promoters influence more strangers towards the brand, eventually creating growth in leads. This can result in better business, better relationships, and a better path to growth.

The Growth Loop Funnel was originally created by Dave McClure, an entrepreneur and angel investor who founded business accelerator, 500 Startups.

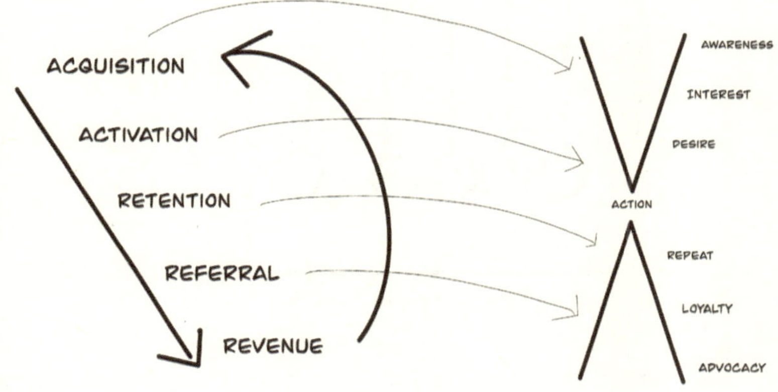

Fig. 7.3: The Growth Loop Funnel.

The model runs on the AARRR framework which comprises Acquisition, Activation, Retention, Referral, and Revenue.

The components in the Flywheel and Growth Loop frameworks are not dissimilar with the flow of the funnel and the shoppers' journey towards becoming customers.

The addition lies in the focus on building a growth continuum and the key to the continuous growth momentum hinges on the "last ball".

THE LAST BALL

The last ball points to the increased focus on customer experience, better products, and better value creations. Small wins across these areas contribute to a continuous growth engine. The exponential growth is a result of the compounding nature of effective growth strategies.

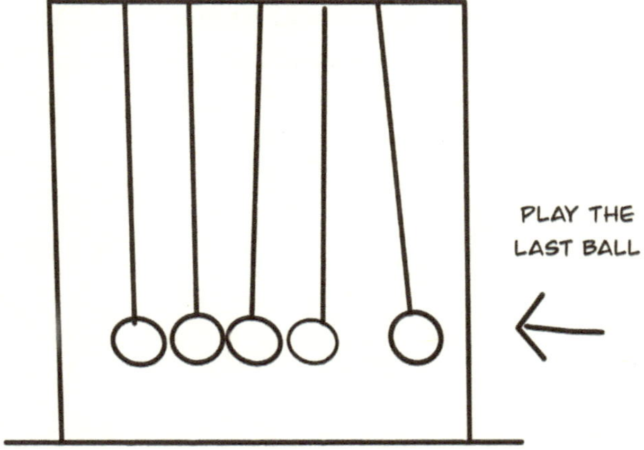

Fig. 7.4: Activate the last ball.

Had the last ball not been hung as a pendulum, or had it been positioned further away from the rest of the balls, it would lack the momentum to sustain the repeat motion.

Here are quite a few examples of those who had played the last ball well. Platforms like Facebook, Snapchat, LinkedIn, Twitter, Instagram, and WhatsApp grew their base through user invitation. The first ball was cast towards the early adopters who started the momentum for growth in user base.

YouTube grows usage of its platform by, first, collecting data on how its user consumes the content. These data points are then fed into machine learning algorithms that create a personalised feed for the user. As the users find more relevant content for consumption, their usage goes up.

Dropbox, on the other hand, designed its product for organic new acquisitions. Sender opens Dropbox apps and sets up an account to deposit documents in its folder. A link to the folder is generated to be sent to the receiver. The receiver goes into the Dropbox platform in order to download the file and is invited to set up an account and download the app.

Dropbox offers its existing users, free storage for linking their Dropbox account to Twitter and Facebook so as to share information about Dropbox. That was a free way to get new users and to grow exponentially.

Facebook has grown to under 3 billion users by encouraging users to add their contacts and sending out emails to those contacts if they are mentioned or tagged on Facebook. These growth hacks helped Facebook to extend its reach organically.

These tactics may start off as experimentations for driving quick conversions, such as how Airbnb piggybacked on Craigslist postings to find homes for short-term lodging or for bed-and-breakfast, and invited them to list on their platform. It was manual and tedious, but it worked, without paid ads, social media, or sophisticated technology.

CREATE YOUR OWN LAST BALL

1 **Develop ideas for continuous sales or usages that do not involve discounts or promotions**
For example, creating reminders based on natural cycles of usage or seasonal needs, providing useful tips on new ways to use the products, etc.

2 **Outline mechanics for referrals that do not involve discounts or promotions**
For example, LinkedIn users are prompted to send invitations to their professional connections. By sharing milestones of completing a course on a LinkedIn profile, users are helping to generate awareness and interest among their connections to check out its learning platform.

3 **Identify tangible channels to continuously engage with customers after sales**
For example, installation of a native app with utility functions that encourage regular usage, in-app purchases for gamification experience, check-ins for periodic product performance review, etc.

4 **Integrate mechanics into the way the product is used**
For example, there are also many references of how online games require their players to broadcast their gaming milestones or invite friends, to earn rewards, and to progress to new levels.

5 **Keep experimenting and improving your growth loops by adding new touchpoints with your user base**
For example, invitations for customers to join closed Telegram channels for more regular updates and conversations, or subscriptions to your Youtube channel.

We are also starting to see brands experimenting with creating a metaverse experience for customer engagement in the virtual world, that could be a possibility too.

CHAPTER 8

MAKING EVERY DOLLAR COUNT

"How should I set my marketing budget?"—this is another common question asked by all marketers, not just by start-ups.

How marketing budgets are allocated really depends on a number of factors:

- the industry that you are in;
- the stage of your business in its market life cycle; as well as
- the size of your business revenue.

STANDARD PERCENTAGE SPEND OVER SALES

A number of articles advocate tabulating marketing budgets based on a percentage of sales. Some suggest it should be 7%, while others advocate 6.5–8.5% and 5–30% ...

But which should it be?

Let's take 7% as a reference.

A new start-up needing to build awareness and establish a base demand is likely to have no revenue or a limited one, let's say $10,000. Hence, it's unrealistic to derive a marketing budget at 7% of the projected $10,000 business revenue, which works out to be only $700. New start-ups are likely to invest a disproportionately high percentage of potential revenue for marketing, sometimes expecting a loss.

Conversely, spending 7% of a $1 billion business revenue on marketing seems extravagant.

I used to manage a portfolio with revenue in the billion dollars level; my marketing budget worked out to be less than 1% of revenue.

There may exist a norm for industry instead of a percentage over revenue. However, this cannot be applied blindly across all companies. It is possible to beat even the norm with the right tactics, to drive better cost efficiency in marketing spend. We will cover some of those in the later part of this chapter.

There is really no magic formula. So, where does one start?

There are a number of ways to construct a marketing budget that makes sense.

BENCHMARKING

In my past budget forecasts, I would use the past year's budget and revenue growth targets as a reference to adjust my forecast accordingly. I would then look at adjusting components based on the assumption and confidence to drive cost efficiency, as well as accommodate for ongoing and new commitments. This, I think, is the easy part.

If you are setting a marketing budget for the first time without the reference of an existing budget, you can make reference to what your competitors in your category are spending since they are probably reaching out to a similar group of target segments.

Bear in mind that the incumbent in the category might have a deeper pocket than you who are just starting out. As such, you should try to refer to the unit economics, such as cost per acquisition (CAC) or value per customer.

In my early years of work, I used to map out competitors' marketing strategies by manually tracking their media tactics and messages. There is more data available today for us to develop a rather convincing reference. For example, if your competitor constantly tops the search listing, it is possible to estimate how much you must spend to get there.

Let's look at an example that has been done.

We had to launch a healthcare service in a new market which has different dynamics from the existing markets we were already operating in. After referencing what the incumbents in the new market had been bidding in paid ads, we estimated that it would cost us $80 per acquisition. From there, we were able to quickly work out the desired budget by factoring in the total number of conversions we wanted.

The $80 per acquisition for the new market was, in fact, higher than what was spent for our existing markets. However, it would have been unrealistic for us to apply the CAC of the existing market for new market entry, as the dynamics in markets differed.

Besides, the projected CAC at $80 was almost double our potential unit revenue ($50) in the new market. That meant we stood to lose money for each acquisition, which would not have been sustainable for the business in the long run.

So, what could be done?

First and foremost, we could reset the marketing budget to align closer to the break-even point, working off a CAC of $50. Up till then, the projected CAC assumed the use of paid ads, which should not be the only tactic for customer acquisition. In this example, by pegging the unit marketing cost ($50) to break-even point at $50, the baseline percentage spend over revenue for brand new start-ups would work out to be 100%.

This is a good example of why the percentage over sales method does not work for new start-ups.

Hence, even after you have established your benchmark, you should always be ready to challenge it. We should explore activating other channels to reduce the reliance on paid ads, such as developing strategic partnerships to access existing pools of ready prospects, as well as to lend credibility to our services.

BOOTSTRAPPED ALLOCATION

This applies mainly to early-stage start-ups.

If you have just seed funding to work with, start by identifying your priority at the start-up stage of development. For example:

- If your immediate priority is prototyping and piloting with potential customer segments, the corresponding marketing cost could be relatively small.

- If your product is ready to launch and it operates in a new economy, chances are your intended target segment may not know how your business works and might not be searching for your solution. You might want to allocate marketing to address your immediate priorities in education and awareness.

You may also adopt a more straightforward budget allocation as a preset share of total available funding allocation in different pockets for product development, hiring, and marketing.

This is when you need to optimise your budget based on the priorities in your marketing and sales funnel. You would want to growth-hack by activating free channels wherever possible, such as PR, partnership, owned outbound sales force, word of mouth, etc.

Your paid marketing would be selective and prioritised for rapid testing.

ALLOCATION BY FUNCTIONS

I had to manage multiple pots of budgets across different business units and different functions, such as branding, sponsorship, channel marketing, product marketing, etc.

Branding-related functions like sponsorship and PR have more predictable allocations according to the commitment of the company towards branding as these have less correlation to revenue generation.

There are multiple paid channels, both offline and online. Offline channels spend is dependent on charges by external media owners and production houses.

Conversely, the budget allocations for online paid channels are within your control. These include paid ads on social media, Google ads, Search Engine Marketing (SEM), app store campaigns, etc.

For these digital channels, you would want to extrapolate their respective past performance data, e.g., cost per conversion, and then use that to project your potential marketing based on your new revenue target.

BUILD FROM PROJECTIONS

Here's a simple example. Let's say your revenue target is set at $500,000, based on the assumption that 500 customers are spending an average of $1,000 each.

Assuming that your (simplistic) funnel performance looked like this:

- You spent $8,000 on your Google ad campaigns to deliver 800 landings (web traffic) onto your website;
- 40 of these paid landings ended up placing an order, which means your conversion rate is 5%, being 40 out of 800. Your CAC will work out to be $200, being $8,000 over 40 orders.

Your increased target for calls is for a total of 50 orders, which means you need to deliver an additional 10 orders. By projecting the same funnel performance, your incremental budget works out to be $2,000, being $200 multiplied by 10. Thus, your revised budget will be $10,000, after adding $2,000 to $8,000.

This is a simplistic way to look at this using only one channel, and it assumes that you are able to generate quality leads that would spend no less than $1,000.

It is, therefore, important to think about where the revenue could come from. We are assuming that all your future revenue comes from new customers and you, therefore, plan your budget according to that.

What if you do not have the luxury of an increased budget—you have to work with $8,000, but the order target continues to climb to 50 orders?

That is where you need to consider expanding your marketing channels and tactics. For example:

- You can diversify new modes of paid ads that might deliver better efficiency, and then test to refine.
- You can activate your existing customers to drive repeat and referrals. Imagine, if you are able to get 10 repeat orders from your existing customers, you will reduce the CAC to $160, instead of $200.

By now, you have improved overall marketing efficiency by reducing the CAC!

If the incremental revenue needs to come from different segments, simply adjust your assumptions on the tactics and their respective cost of acquisition.

Essentially, when you build your budget from ground up, you will find yourself at a stronger position to defend and augment your budget.

In doing so, you are making a marketing budget an investment towards your goal. It is not just an expenditure.

UNDERSTANDING ZERO-BASED BUDGETING (ZBB)

It is possible that the previous allocation of budget is being questioned and you are required to propose a baseline budget. As such, all projected spend must be justified for the new period.

I have been in such a situation where each country's team was given a baseline bootstrapped budget allocation.

Any request for an incremental budget had to be justified according to their respective need and it had to be pegged to the projected revenue.

ZBB does not mean working with zero budget. But rather, starting with a "zero base" without reference to past allocation. Every function within the organisation is analysed for its needs and costs. Apply the principles from "Allocation by Functions" and "Building from Projections" as shared earlier.

Let me illustrate.

In the past budget year, we may have had a budget of $10,000, of which, $3,000 went to social media, $5,000 to paid Google ads, and $2,000 for collaterals.

ZBB would require us to first define our marketing goals. If the new budget year requires us to use the same amount to support co-marketing activities with a new strategic partner, which could double the leads. We might have less reliance on paid ads and can scale back on the investment in that pocket.

STRETCHING YOUR MARKETING DOLLARS

Two weeks into my marketing leadership role at honestbee, I was told that the budget needed to be revised downward significantly, by as much as 70%, across the eight markets we operated in.

We had to show that the business ran with steady traction even in the absence of marketing.

A little background on honestbee. Its core business was to provide delivery services for food and grocery, but it also collected and delivered laundry, served B2B clients with concierge and parcel delivery services.

There were other more established competitors in the same categories, with deeper pockets, such as Deliveroo and Foodpanda.

Paid marketing was a major part of its marketing. Our tall order of the day was to maintain revenue level at a significantly reduced marketing budget level.

Assess the Spend

The first thing we did was to assess the distribution of the (budget) burn. Due to the nature of the business, some spends were still necessary to sustain the demand but there were potential wastages that went on unnoticed.

Indeed, we subsequently discovered that e-coupons were used on a big scale to entice new orders, and these redemptions were counted as marketing costs. However, because no caps were set over the tenure of redemptions, the redemptions were eating into most of our reduced allocated budget!

Something had to be done fast to stop a leaking tap!

Stop the Burn

We immediately took stock of the live e-coupons that were issued more than four weeks before that were still sitting in customers' app wallets. Many of them were way past the promotional periods but were still not deactivated as there wasn't enough diligence in monitoring the coupon validity. Customers could effectively redeem these even if they were no longer valid.

These were immediately made invalid and the customer service team was notified. Instead of a blanket issuance to both existing and new customers, we also reprioritised the issuance of coupons towards the acquisition of new customers.

However, coupons might have worked earlier to drive new orders but it was simply not sustainable for us to continue eroding our margin for every order. The use of coupons was subsequently rationalised—setting limits to the tenure of the coupons as well as to who they are issued to. We also implemented regular check-ins for coupon expiries.

Harvest Insights for Actions

As we dived into our customer data to better understand how people were using our services, we found out that a significant portion of our existing grocery delivery customers were re-ordering from us, without using any coupons. That is a visible sign of customer loyalty.

There was no need for us to make further cuts to our margin by giving coupons and, hence, we could reserve the coupons to encourage new customers for trials.

We also learnt that the grocery delivery customers tended to be loyal to their preferred grocers. As such, we could trigger more purchase instances by simply spotlighting offers that were originally set up by the grocers.

And it worked.

As we studied the Gross Merchandise Value (GMV) contribution for the grocery delivery vertical from different markets, we discovered that in most markets, the Pareto principle still applied.

A core handful of grocery merchants were delivering as much as two-thirds of the revenue for that business vertical. This meant that we should focus our effort to maintain the volume from these grocers. These groups of grocers also had loyal followings of customers and hence, it made sense for us to tap into their platforms and touchpoints to raise awareness and drive usage for our deliveries, at a relatively low or no cost.

With these, not only were we able to significantly control wastage in marketing spends, we were uncovering new channels to drive new leads and new tactics for growing repeat orders.

In addition, we managed to augment our digital marketing campaigns to reach prospects with similar profiles as our higher value customers. Our social media marketing was refocused towards time belts that yielded us high order sizes.

Activating Free Channels

With less resources available at our disposal, we started to look at other means to drive revenue, and there were quite a few levers we could pull to reach new people and to drive conversions. Plus, our in-app notifications continued to be useful for prompting actions, at no additional cost.

Strategic marketing partnership provided a great avenue for us to tap onto funding for co-marketing activities as well as to access new clusters of potential new target audiences. We also steered away from hefty co-funding of food delivery promotions. Instead, we focused on providing more airtime to those food merchants who were prepared to fund discounts from their end.

We pitched media stories with the press to talk about food trends and interesting new products from our merchants. These were crafted to align with and appeal to the content directions by lifestyle sections of the main press, as well as lifestyle platforms.

One more thing which we did not do enough of was to engage our existing customers purposefully. Instead of blanket EDMs (Electronic Direct Mail) marketing, we became more selective with offers and promotions.

Investing Where It Mattered

Creativity abounded when we had little funds.

We had taken a bunch of actions to help us significantly cut our reliance on paid marketing and activate free channels. With more funds freed up and a better understanding of our performance market baselines, our in-market teams were able to pitch and justify any increase in their marketing budgets. At the end of the day, we were in a much better position to meet our monthly targets for the subsequent months while operating smarter with less budget.

KEEP REVENUE PIPELINES IN SIGHT

Growth at all cost is no longer in fashion.

Recent occurrences of lacklustre tech IPOs (initial public offerings) and overvaluations of start-ups cause the investors to shift their focus towards capital efficiency, unit economics, margin, and profitability.

The book, *The Minimalist Entrepreneur*, advocates that start-ups not to be in a hurry to spend, but instead think about how to stay profitable by making calculated spends, decreasing the deficit, reducing the unnecessary burn, and being in less of a hurry to hire a big team.

In the first place, I find it unthinkable that any business could sustain without a steady stream of revenue pipelines. Even when you have a new injection of funds, monitor your burn and make sure you have visible sales pipelines.

Know where your revenue might be coming from and construct your sales and marketing plan to pursue those channels.

BUILD YOUR MARKETING BUDGET

Use the answers from these questions to build your proposal for a marketing budget.

1. What are your revenue targets in the next six months or one year?
2. How much of your revenue is confirmed? This would refer to those customers who had made a commitment by means of confirmed bookings or contracts, as well as expected re-orders from existing customers. By deducting the "confirmed revenue" from your revenue target, you would get the "unconfirmed revenue".
3. Out of the "unconfirmed revenue" amount, which pipelines are you working on and what is the expected size of these revenues?
4. Out of the "unconfirmed revenue" amount, what is the revenue gap after deducting "identified pipelines"?
5. How would you deliver these revenue pots from your answers to questions 2, 3, and 4 through strategic partnerships, sales and marketing, etc.?

DECIPHERING MARKETING ROI

This is an age-old quote by departmental store mogul John Wanamaker: "Half the money I spend on advertising is wasted; the trouble is I don't know which half."

P&G's FMOT (first mentioned in Chapter 6) refers to the first 3–5 seconds when a shopper notices an item in a retail environment. It suggests that running advertising does not guarantee purchase as there are distractions even at the point of sales.

We know full well that the consumers' path to purchase is not linear. They have choices and there are distractions before they finally buy a product or service.

In the current era of big data, dynamic analytics that come with digital marketing promise more ways to quantify marketing success and its causation. As such, there is an ongoing expectation for marketing leaders, not just resource-crunched and fund-tight start-ups, to justify marketing investment, report, and be accountable to the management team leadership.

So, why do marketing leaders struggle with reporting marketing return on investment (ROI)?

AN OVER SIMPLISTIC VIEW OF INVESTMENT AND REVENUE ATTRIBUTION

We know that multiple components are at play at different stages of the customer journey and not all components have the same degree of impact on sales conversion.

Let me illustrate. Angela searched for potential destinations for a quick getaway with a close friend. Her search results page for "short island getaways" showed a few listings of nearby holiday resorts as well as blogs elaborating on the top 10 short getaways. Among them was a glamping resort (GR) recently featured in the lifestyle section of the local newspaper. The press article documented the journalist's personal experience as a guest and her review of the resort.

Angela clicked on the listing of images from the search ranking page to explore its website, but she did not make any booking.

Later that evening, when she was browsing through her social media platform, she saw an ad for GR. The same thing would recur in the next couple of days, whenever she went onto her social media platform.

A week later, when she was ready to book her short vacation and was browsing the reviews for her potential shortlists on TripAdvisor, GR was now at the top of her mind.

She eventually went on to an Online Travel Agent (OTA) and booked the glamping resort as there was an attractive offer tied to payment made with her Mastercard.

There were multiple touchpoints where Angela encountered GR and they all played a part in coaxing her to eventually make a booking with them. It's clear that the GR marketing team had been busy with a line-up of marketing tactics implemented.

Table 9.1 maps out the tactics deployed at each channel by the GR team.

Channel	Tactics	Funnel Stage	Cost
Search Engine Optimisation (SEO)—so that GR's URL would surface in relevant searches	Built backlink with popular travel, lifestyle review sites; incorporated keywords into the site content; refined loading speed of the web page.	Middle	Internal
Search Marketing (SEM)	Bought listings of GR URL to be visible on search results of selective keywords.	Middle	Paid ads
Blogs and Press Features	Seeded influencers and media on the GR experience by inviting them for complimentary stays at the resort. The stays were accompanied by curated treatment, activities, and media kits.	Top	Internal cost for complimentary stay
Social Media Re-targeting Ads	Ensured that there were pop-up ads and listings on social media to reach those who had visited the GR site earlier but did not book.	Middle	Paid
Tripadvisor	Invited guests to post positive reviews on Tripadvisor and similar review sites.	Middle	Internal cost for incentives
Online Travel Agent Sites	Offered promotion to incentivise immediate booking.	Bottom	Internal cost for promotion

Table 9.1: Tactics deployed at each funnel stage.

Each of these components played a role in the buying journey.

A simplistic view of Return on Investment (ROI) is usually referred to as Revenue per Spend.

In reality, this following might be true: Return on Investment has to be a function of initiatives across driving awareness, conversions and repeats.

ROI = f [(awareness) + (conversion) + (repeat)]

NOT MEASURING THE RIGHT METRICS

Tracking the right metrics at different stages of the funnel is vital not just for reporting the effectiveness of marketing efforts, but also useful for refining marketing efficiency and optimising marketing spend. There are, in fact, many data points to review and tools to do so. Hence, it's easy to get paralysis by analysis if you do not know what to look for.

Here are the two key sets of metrics to navigate.

ROI Metrics

These are the ones we would typically report to management as they relate to how marketing dollars are spent and the value it generates. Key measurements include:

- Cost per acquisition (CAC);
- Revenue per customer; and
- Customer lifetime value (CLTV).

Funnel Metrics

As outlined in Table 9.2 (overleaf), these analyse how the components at different stages of the funnel perform. They are more relevant for the marketing team in refining their strategy and justifying specific tactics.

Top of the Funnel (ToFU)	Middle of the Funnel (MoFU)	Bottom of the Funnel (BoFU)
Metrics measure the prospect behaviours. (These data points can be derived from the platform analytics.)	Metrics that show how leads are moving from awareness to consideration and how they are showing interest in your product and services. (These data points are most likely found in your owned platforms.)	Metrics that measure when the shoppers decide to be a customer by committing to an order. (These data points are most likely found in your owned platforms.)
Examples: • web impressions • site traffic from organic search and paid search • average time on site • bounce rates • social media metrics— which contents drive stronger engagement rates	Examples: • subscriptions for your newsletter or collaterals • app downloads • email engagement • inbound calls or WhatsApp enquiry	Examples: • free trials • demo requests

Table 9.2: Funnel metrics.

In order to improve marketing ROI, start by analysing the funnel performance to determine how to shorten the sale cycle, and get more shoppers to progress through the funnel into becoming customers.

DECIPHERING VANITY METRIC

Not all measurable data points are meaningful, or useable as important indicators for effectiveness of your marketing efforts. It is possible to be distracted by *vanity metrics* that are essentially data that look satisfying on paper, but they don't really move the needles for your business goals.

Some common examples of vanity metric include:

- Number of social media followers

A sizeable social media follower base serves little purpose if these followers show little interest to engage in conversations with the brand or its community. As such, engagement rates like click-through, comments, and data on reshare of social media content are more meaningful.

Through these, we have a better understanding of what our community is interested in and if our content is valuable. All these can contribute towards building an emotional connection with its target audience.

- App downloads

If the growth in app download is accompanied by a high app uninstall rate, it would mean that the marketing investment is wasted. As such, it makes more sense to measure app retention which is simply total app download minus the app uninstall.

Monitoring in-app behaviour can help us understand how people are using the app as well as clues to why they might choose to uninstall.

MARKETING ROI REPORTING

1 Measure what you need to report—include your key ROI metrics and funnel metrics.
2 Be selective about what you report—focus on telling a story about how your business is doing and how effective your marketing strategy is.
3 Focus on actionable metrics instead vanity metrics—actionable metrics are ones that demonstrate clear cause and effect.

CHAPTER 10

BUILDING THE RIGHT TEAM

How should your marketing team evolve as your business needs change? Should you hire or train? Let's look at how this works for companies in three different phases.

THE BOOTSTRAPPED PHASE

Most founders of early-stage start-ups and small business owners, working with limited resources and funding, are likely to take on multiple roles including the marketing function.

As many of them might not be trained in marketing, they could consult advisors or mentors on the overall strategic direction. Thereafter, they may consider outsourcing specialised services, such as PR, copywriting, design, and complex production work, etc.

Other day-to-day marketing operations like social media pages, simple digital ad buys, content and collateral creation, can be handled with the help of junior marketing hands or be supported by interns. However, while interns make for affordable hires, they may not be accessible throughout the year.

THE GROWTH PHASE

As the companies grow, business owners might want to start appointing someone to take care of marketing functions specifically, so that they can focus on other aspects of growth in technical and operational functions, securing additional funding, and strategic business partnerships.

At this stage, the marketing lead would be expected to:
- Plan and manage marketing campaigns;
- Plan and manage social media content calendars;
- Set up digital ad buys on Google/Facebook;
- Develop collaterals and content;
- Manage media relations;
- Manage marketing partnerships;
- Run event marketing;
- Send out EDMs; and
- Respond to customer complaints and reviews on social media, app stores, and Google business pages.

As work volume increases, the appointed marketing lead may need a support team to help maintain day-to-day operations like social media page management and digital campaign ad buys. These support functions could comprise full-time hires as well as interns.

Resourcing can be more complicated when there is more than one market. Additional considerations would include:
- Should there be duplicate roles in localised markets?
- What role should remain as centralised shared services?

Always right-size the marketing team to align with business objectives. For businesses serving B2B customers, additional functions for account management and partnership development need to be built as well.

THE SCALED-UP PHASE

When I inherited a small team in my first marketing leadership role, their main functions were primarily to support weekly retail promotions, in-store merchandising, and collaterals. Over time, it expanded to accommodate added functions like digital marketing, social media, branding, sponsorships, reward programmes, etc. As my company started to introduce more retail banners, I had to start catering for different tracks of marketing activities for each retail channel.

In my other leadership roles, there was added complexity of multiple markets and functions where I had to think about deployment of centralised shared services to support multiple markets as well as balancing the needs for localised functions.

Fig. 10.1 provides a simplified overview of the different roles that a big marketing organisation might include.

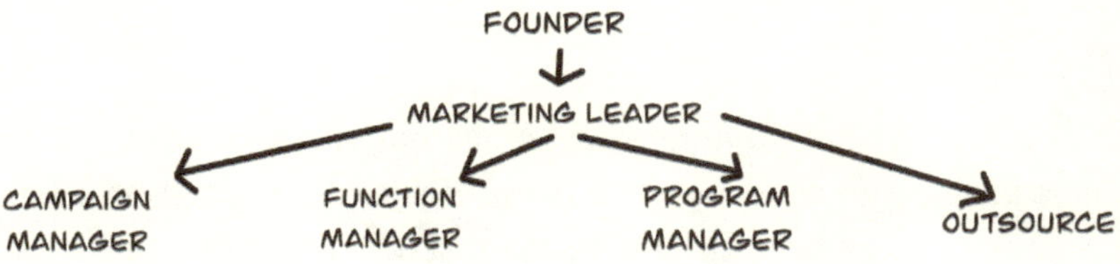

Fig. 10.1: Potential role categories in big marketing organisations.

First, the campaign managers' roles may be similar as those described in the earlier phases—they are the point persons for planning and managing marketing campaigns. However, there could be dedicated ones appointed to take care of the needs of different business verticals. These managers may have support staff depending on the size of their respective portfolios.

There are also shared "Functions" and "Programmes" that are likely to be centralised.

"Functions" roles refer to specialised marketing functions requiring pre-training in those disciplines, such as corporate communication and media relations, creative or design, performance marketing, consumer insights, etc. "Programmes" roles refer to loyalty programmes, membership programmes, closed community of customers, etc. In larger companies, these teams may comprise talents from multiple disciplines.

For example, if your business owns a loyalty programme, you may need help to:

- Acquire new enrolments into your programme;
- Plan and implement the issuance and redemption of points;
- Sign up merchants and suppliers to provide products or services for the redemption of points;
- Manage customer enquiries and complaints on usage of the loyalty programme;
- Run analysis of the cost and revenue for the running of the programme; and
- Monitor and report performance for usage and breakage of loyalty points.

When the programme is at its nascent stage, these might be manageable by one person or a team as this can be a full-time job.

Let's look at an example of marketing resourcing consideration.

Jay runs an all-in-one Voice over Internet Protocol (VoIP) business phone system that helps small businesses generate leads and track performance for inbound calls, sales calls and automated cold call campaigns.

The company had just secured seed funding and even though he was instrumental and hands-on in acquiring his first customers, Jay needed someone to help with new customer acquisition and digital marketing. With his hiring budget, he is only able to pay for half of what a mid-weight talent is paid in the market to help him plan and grow his customer base.

Jay could only afford to hire a junior marketing person with little experience on marketing strategy and campaign planning. His predicament is not unique among early-stage start-ups, and is often applicable for the scale-ups as well.

So what are his options?

- **Hire and train**

  Hire someone who can do a generalist job, but who demonstrates an affinity for his business category, has a good attitude, and with the hunger to learn.

  Thereafter, Jay can consider sending this person for specialised training on digital marketing campaign set-ups. The investment for training is one-off but it will reap longer term benefits in strengthening marketing capability and talent retention.

  Jay can also identify this person from someone within his existing team who shows similar attributes and can be appointed as marketing lead designate. This is a great option as the insider would have a short learning curve having known the working of the business.

- **Build, Transfer, and Operate (BTO)**

  Jay could enlist the help of a boutique service provider for a limited amount of time to help him build the strategy and plan, with the intent to transfer the know-how to his identified marketing lead, where they would eventually be able to operate on their own.

  As Jay's business grows, he would adopt a similar approach for his other functions.

There are occasions where you have to decide between hiring external talents and building these capabilities in-house. You might also consider just outsourcing to external service providers.

HIRE, BUILD, OR OUTSOURCE

Here are the reasons for hiring, building and outsourcing talents. They are applicable across multiple functions, not just marketing:

HIRE (External Talents)	BUILD (In-House Capabilities)	OUTSOURCE (Consultants or Service Providers)
• There is critical mass and volume for specialty functions and the person needs to work closely with other internal stakeholders. • There is a need for high responsiveness and turnaround. • The role deals with information that might be sensitive and private, such as customer personal data. However, the fixed cost of maintaining an in-house talent base could be expensive.	• Talent understands the company's challenges and is familiar with the company's systems and processes. However, the capabilities for the required roles might be absent in the company. External training might be required and that could take time.	• Allows for flexibility in deployment especially when the need for these functions is seasonal and ad hoc. • The required function needs pre-training, prior experience, and track records, currently not available in the organisation However, it can be costly to appoint external consultants especially when these service providers have complex value chains requiring them to charge higher fees. Work scope is also expected to be relatively well-defined and any incremental requests may come at additional costs.

AFTERWORD

Every business is different. This book may not tell you what direction you should be heading; it serves to help you find the answers. This is not a textbook, as my intention was to make it a make-it-simpler book with many examples, stories, and lessons to help you navigate marketing and branding for your business to go to market.

The best way to use the book is to apply the learning and investigate the thought starters.

If I were to project into the future, this is what I would like to see you approach your go-to market strategy

You might have identified a problem and you might have an idea to solve it.

You know to sharpen your business idea by defining the need such that people are willing to pay for your proposed solution. To do this well, you set out to understand your potential target segment, such as where to find them, how to address them, and how to pitch to them.

You know how to go about validating it with the right group of people and build a strong value proposition to commercialise it. With a validated idea, you know how to go about building your pitch for investors because you know what they are looking for.

When you are ready to launch, you know how to reach out to your potential customers. You know how to gather insights on what they might be thinking at every stage of the buying journey and how they make decisions. As such, you are able to speak to their needs and leverage different media to engage and communicate with them.

You set out to differentiate yourself from your competition and you are able to move your prospects through the chaotic middle ground of research and comparison closer to the decision point.

After fighting off the competition to secure interest from your prospect, you are able to remove potential obstacles and address the perceived risk to finally make them say "yes" to you.

You will remove friction and stress from the buying process by fixing technical and logistic glitches that might hinder.

When all that goes well, your potential lead becomes a customer. Congratulations!

However, you know your job does not end there.

You rally the whole organisation to work together to keep these customers returning and be loyal to your brand, it would be great that they eventually become advocates for you.

You set your growth engine in motion because your growth needs to come from both your existing customers and new ones. You would continue to experiment, measure, refine, and then pivot.

You are no longer intimidated and confused. You know enough to find your way without getting more confused in the process as you practise to build business muscle memories, ready to flex to new challenges, to stay agile, to adapt and evolve, and to win.

You are ready and set to go! You are ready for the market!

Along the way when you are confused, you can always reach out to me at: https://www.linkedin.com/in/thechrisspeak/

ACKNOWLEDGEMENTS

This book is a milestone for my career—a career which started off with passion for creativity and perfected over the years for a greater purpose.

For starting well, my gratitude goes to **Kate James.**

In my early days in the advertising industry as a small fish in the big ocean, Kate was the person who opened my eyes to the possibilities. She was Creator Director and General Manager at the advertising agency, JWT Direct. I caught her attention as "the girl with the feisty tenacity" because I wouldn't give up under the tyranny of a particular client. She was a boss and mentor, who eventually became a friend.

She turned on my switch to the craft of advertising, literally. I discovered that she was the brains behind the marketing campaign which inspired me to join the creative industry.

The best advice she gave me was to devote two years to learning the craft of direct marketing, a move that was seen—and mocked— by my peers as me leaving the glamour of "above-the-line" agencies that create visible TV commercials, splashy print ads. To that, she assured me that I would emerge better than the rest of my peers from the "above-the-line" discipline. And she was right.

My first award-winning campaign, "Gentlemen, Lift Your Skirts", was also birthed under her leadership.

From her, I learnt how the human mind works at different stages of opening a direct mailer and how the right messages on every component of the envelope, cover letter, brochure, and response mailer, could trigger actions, and how a well-constructed letter could touch hearts and move emotion.

My mind had been trained to apply the same microscopic lens into building funnel communications, customer journey mapping, and user experience design in the years that followed.

She believed in me.

My journey to growth has been paved with these great leaders who believed in me.

- To **Lim Sau Hoong** whose name has been associated with many memorable TV commercials, for her recognition and unconditional support in the recent years of my personal growth. She has been a great role model, as one with great humility despite her many achievements. I have also been greatly blessed by her friendship.
- To **Mike Stepan**, then CEO of Publicis in Singapore, who was a nurturing mentor and a father figure during a challenging period of my life.
- To my ex-boss and then CEO of NTUC FairPrice, **Seah Kian Peng**, who supported my unorthodox ideas to break new ground in branding and marketing. He had the foresight to endorse my pursuits for digital transformation initiatives and excellence.

My appreciation goes to **Hau Koh Foo** and **Shirley Wong**, from Singapore Management University Institute of Innovation and Entrepreneurship, for the opportunity to contribute to the start-up eco-system.

A shout-out to my fellow teams and colleagues over the years who stood together with me at the frontlines of many battles and challenges, without which there would be no growth.

The idea for this book was conceived over two years ago and is now made a reality.

Thanks to **Phoon Kok Hwa**, my publisher, for guiding me on building the concept for the book, setting the cadence for writing my manuscript, and cheering me to complete the race.

Last but not least, my gratitude goes to **The Almighty God** for the gifts and talents from above, for sending these wonderful angels who have inspired and enriched my life.

ABOUT THE AUTHOR

CHRISTINA LIM has had an exciting career that spans over three decades. Starting in the creative industry, she subsequently spent more than 10 years in marketing and branding leadership roles, overseeing both local and regional portfolios. She has been intimately involved in the start-up community, as advisor and leader for start-ups and scale-ups. As CMO-In-Residence with Singapore Management University Institute of Innovation and Entrepreneurship, she has mentored and advised over 80 early-stage start-ups on their go-to market strategies.

She has an in-depth understanding of the needs and challenges of start-ups at different stages of their growth, and her advice covers branding, business models and funnel strategies, as well as consumer tech product marketing. She is a thought leader who speaks regularly at conferences across a wide array of subjects including retail, e-commerce, branding, marketing, trends, and leadership.

BIBLIOGRAPHY

Balfour, Brian. "Growth Loops are the New Funnels." *Reforge*. https://www.reforge.com/blog/growth-loops.

Bowie, David. "The Verbasizer." *YouTube*. https://www.youtube.com/watch?v=x3IKLMgFaDA.

Chatterjee, Dipanjan. "A Pragmatic Guide To Brand Value." *Forbes*. 6 August 2019. https://www.forbes.com/sites/forrester/2019/08/06/a-pragmatic-guide-to-brand-value/?sh=51dd1a53436c.

Cliffe, Callum. "What are the Top 10 Most Recognisable Brands in the World?" *IG*. https://www.ig.com/sg/trading-strategies/what-are-the-top-10-most-recognisable-brands-in-the-world--200217.

Cook, Alex, et al. "Evolving the Google Identity: A New Brand Identity Makes Google More Accessible and Useful to Our Users." *Google Design*. https://design.google/library/evolving-google-identity/.

Morgan, Adam. *Eating the Big Fish: How Challenger Brands Can Compete Against Brand Leaders*. Hoboken, NJ: John Wiley & Sons, 2009.

Robertson, Graham. *Beloved Brands: The Playbook for How to Build a Brand Your Consumers Will Love*. Scotts Valley, CA: CreateSpace Independent Publishing Platform, 2018.

Sun, Tzu. *The Art of War*. Translated by John Minford, New York, NY: Viking. 2002.

"The Top 12 Reasons Startups Fail." *CB Insights*. 3 August 2021. https://www.cbinsights.com/research/startup-failure-reasons-top/.

"The Value Proposition Canvas." *Strategyzer*. https://www.strategyzer.com/canvas/value-proposition-canvas.

Weinberg, Gabriel, and Justin Mares. *Traction: How Any Startup Can Achieve Explosive Customer Growth*. New York, NY: Portfolio/Penguin, 2015.